Out Of Focus

By *John J. Larish*

The story of how Kodak lost its direction.

Technology had been his previous company's business. Can he change Kodak cultures? The photo digital world wakes up on his watch.

Another Kodak insider CEO takes over. He hires a technology president.

Kodak's technology president becomes the CEO. His printer-focused vision misses numerous image business opportunities already in place at Kodak.

The often asked question, will Kodak survive? Selling patents and licenses is a shallow well that will run dry.

Introduction

The name Kodak was a household word for more than a hundred years, but in recent years it has been surpassed as a brand name by electronic and digital companies like Sony and Microsoft. For over two decades the Eastman Kodak Company has been a challenge both to the company itself with the extreme change of direction of its basic photography business and to investors as well.

Once a part of the Dow Index—today, little heed is paid to Kodak unless its investment rating is dropped again or more severe financial constraints develop like bankruptcy.

Over the last thirty-five years, seven different chief executive officers have tried to find solid ground for this company, but today it has a small fraction of the employees that it had at the start of that period and many challenges that are still unsolved.

My personal story of working in the photo industry and at Kodak took me through some valuable positions. The path to Kodak for me was not an easy or direct one. After Korean War service, I visited Rochester looking for employment, but Kodak was not ready for me. After working in both television broadcasting and then managing a photofinishing lab (one of the early independent color print photofinishing labs and that experience is another interesting story by itself), in 1959, I was offered a job as a technical sales representative by Ansco, Kodak's only real competitor in the United States at that time.

From a technical sales representative in Indiana and Kentucky, I moved on to calling on places like the Strategic Air Command (SAC) in Nebraska, Hallmark Cards, and other large locations in the middle part of the United States; then I became a district manager in California. To my surprise, when I reapplied to Kodak, I was hired, but not without some legal questions on the part of GAF (Ansco) attorneys.

Kodak brought me wide experiences ranging from arranging customer training and conducting color processes classes overseas, customer service management, international markets covering Africa, Middle East and Japan, and finally senior market intelligence which allowed me to bring the developments in electronics and other new technologies at the beginning of the 1980s to the attention of thousands of people within the Kodak family.

Data that I had been collecting for years helped Alecia Swasy with her 1997 book, *Changing Focus*; the story of Kodak's trying to change from a chemical company to a digital company. My own first book after I retired, *Understanding Electronic Photography*, has become a fixture on many litigators' desks because of the extensive coverage of the field at the time of publication. Today many companies look to intellectual property as a significant source of income and one that, over the years, was identified by Kodak as a source of future profits.

It has been a challenge to put together all of the pieces that make up the story of the Eastman Kodak Company. For almost three dozen years after my retirement from Kodak, I have been a Kodak watcher. In addition to reporting on local radio and television, my articles have appeared in the local press as well as in national and international publications. It was interesting to look back at the articles of ten and twenty years ago that pointed out some of the concerns at Kodak. The business and financial challenges began for Kodak many more years ago than most people realize.

The Photo Marketing Association International invited me to present programs at the beginning of the '90s that talked about electronic imaging as the industry's future partner. With this unique perspective, it's interesting to see that some parts of Kodak, particularly its graphic printing area, have returned to the game plan of a few years ago. It is not hard to see why some people call Kodak "HP East". Kodak's current CEO as well as many other major roles was filled by people who came to Kodak from HP and have already left Kodak. The change in cultures, from one company to another is and has been a great challenge.

Documents about Kodak make up my personal file of more than 20,000 pages that have been collected from many sources. Paper files are sometimes easier and faster to peruse than digital files. Many hours have been spent interviewing people both inside and outside of Kodak. These interviews have provided further insights into the how and why of the world of photography, Kodak's world, changed rapidly and dramatically. Trying to cover all the parts of the Kodak story was like trying to put your arms around the heaviest person you have ever met...

There is no way to repay all those people who have taken time to share their experiences and thoughts from years gone by. All that I can say is deepest thanks to each and every one of you.

The dramatic change from the original analog world to a digital world has had a great impact on Kodak and many other companies around the globe. Will a great old company like Eastman Kodak with its more than 100 years of history survive? There are no certainties in life and the future fate of Kodak is still a question mark.

The story of Kodak is a story that needed telling. We learn from experiences and hopefully another generation will have learned from what has happened at Kodak. Long term strategic planning will not satisfy the short returns desired by today's financial community. It is true that the corporation is responsible only to the stockholders, but every company is multi-dimensional with stockholders, employees and customers forming three legs of a stool. If you short-change any of the three legs, the stool will topple. We have seen this happen over and over again.

Stockholders must allow management to build the company, yet it must be built responsibly without taking short cuts just to fix the quarterly bottom line. Care must be taken not to lose **customer focus**. Then there is the need for loyal, dedicated employees who are willing to spend the extra hours which will build a company to greatness. Today, it is not a 9 to 5 world of the Kodak of bygone years. Customer service can no longer be neglected and not simply covered by a Web site in which everything must be deciphered by the customer.

Kodak has gone from a company that was at the top of the world and it is now facing its own "perfect storm." Today, all of the legs of Kodak's stool have been affected and a very uneven company has resulted. Kodak's CEO is at risk of falling from the unbalanced stool. Kodak now faces an uncertain future. It is out of focus and if it is saved as anything but a product name, it will be a surprise to investors, but it will be unhappy news to Kodak employees and to its loyal customers. Investors are genuinely concerned while employees face uncertainty and customers feel abandonment.

John J. Larish

Chapter One—The Ghost of Kodak Past

The story of Kodak begins more than 100 years ago when a junior bank clerk in his early 20s, George Eastman, became interested in photography. While working in his job at the Rochester (New York) Savings Bank, he spent evenings trying to simplify the wet plate process of that time.

Since England was where much of the development of photography was happening, Eastman took a trip there in

1879. When he returned home, he and a friend formed a partnership known as the Eastman Dry Plate Company. The company was so successful that six months later George Eastman was on his way to becoming one of America's great entrepreneurs.

Pictures of Eastman smiling are rare; this young man came from a challenged background. His

George Eastman Age 36

father died when George was eight and his dry plate business almost failed when spots began to appear in the emulsions produced by the company. The problem was

First Kodak camera 1888

later traced to the animal gelatin that was made in New England.

George never stopped researching and inventing. His greatest efforts were putting emulsions on film base. However, it was almost a quarter century before a patent lawsuit was settled over the invention of the roll film. Hannibal Goodwin, who had already died, was credited with the invention that Eastman had already made into a successful product.

Eastman was ever innovative. When the Eastman Theater in Rochester, New York, was being built, the theater builders noticed that the areas around the upper balconies were poorly lighted. When George Eastman visited the site, he was told about the problem and he came up with an innovative solution.

He had them take round, galvanized wash buckets about 4 feet across, install lights inside of the buckets and hang these from the ceiling as indirect lighting fixtures for that area. Painted gold, the hanging wash buckets can still be seen today in the Kodak Theater (recently renamed) in Rochester.

Eastman worked hard and played hard. He enjoyed hunting trips to Africa and visits to South America and other parts of the world that were potential markets for his growing business. He is remembered for encouraging employees.

Rochester was always home to George Eastman as was the beautiful house that he built on East Avenue for his mother. Stories about the house and its magnificent organ that entertained Eastman each morning during breakfast were just a few of the legends that have passed down over the years about Eastman.

Many 1920 summer mornings George Eastman would choose to walk from his home on East Avenue to his Kodak headquarters on State Street. His chauffeur would follow with the car, but for George it was an invigorating way to start the day. His path took him past St. Joseph Catholic Church where he would always pull out his pocket watch to check the time against the tower clock.

One day he saw that the clock had stopped. As soon as he got to the office, he sent a check for $100 to the church to repair the clock; even a detail as small as a clock didn't miss George's attention.

Once called the Image Center of the World, Rochester, New York, today actually has more people in the educational community than are employed in the imaging world. Twenty-one community colleges, colleges, and universities, are located in Rochester or in the surrounding communities. These schools have over 89,000 full-time and part-time students and employ almost 8,700 faculty and over 32,000 other workers.

Two of the best known and largest are the University of Rochester and RIT (Rochester Institute of Technology). RIT was best known just a few years ago for its photography and printing schools, but now the university has significant imaging science, microelectronic engineering, biotechnology education and other programs. Recently, RIT added an information technology college and major programs in sustainability.

The universities and colleges in the Rochester area cover all possible disciplines, but you have to wonder why more of the young people don't stay in Rochester. Attractive offers from Sun Belt communities and marketing centers certainly have been a drawing card for the graduating seniors. On the other hand, over and over you hear of former students moving back to Rochester because it's where they want to raise their families.

Rochester may be a complete unknown location to some people, but for entrepreneurs, in past years, it has been a good place for developing businesses. Companies like Kodak, Xerox, Bausch & Lomb and Jell-O, are only a few of the names that began in Rochester and have reached international prominence.

Originally, Rochester was known as the Flour City because of the water-powered flour mills and the Erie Canal that ran through the heart of the city. Today it is known as the Flower City because of the beautiful spring Lilac Festival that brings hundreds of thousands of people to Rochester each year.

One topic that will not raise any eyebrows in Rochester is the weather. An old joke says that George Eastman chose Rochester as his base city for starting the Eastman Kodak Company because it had so many days of 18% gray skies. That particular shade of gray has been used for many years to measure the quality of images.

Rochester has four beautiful seasons and such beautiful flora that it is hard to believe that the winters are as difficult as they often can be. The reality is that most of the large cities in the northwest part of New York State--Buffalo, Rochester, and Syracuse--are all challenged by winter weather each year and it is an annual race to see which city has the most snow. In spite of that, the Rochester airport remains open more than Chicago's O'Hare Airport.

Some neighborhoods in Rochester still carry the names of the ethnic groups that originally settled them, like Germantown. It is easy to think of Rochester as a community of churches since there are so many Protestant,

Catholic, Islamic and Jewish houses of worship, many with close connections to ethnic communities.

Kodak was known as a WASP company (White, Anglo Saxon, Protestant) until 1964 when the quiet streets of Rochester became the scene of race riots. Black young people were unemployed and took to the streets to make their voices heard.

Many people were surprised when the city of Rochester in 1964 faced the challenge of race riots—it was truly an unsettling time for everyone in the community. Over 60 hours in July 1964, four people were killed, 350 injured and there was more than a million dollars in property damage. Now Eastman Kodak and other Rochester companies of today have been recognized for their diversity leadership both racially and sexually.

Rochester had been dubbed "Smugtown" in the 1950s because of the complacency of local companies, large and small. There was economic prosperity and amicable labor/management relations for the white community while the black community was left behind in poor neighborhoods. Political channels had not worked so the arrest of an allegedly drunk and disorderly African-American man triggered the riots.

Today, while city schools, in many cases, may have a predominance of minority groups, the suburban schools are mostly well mixed. Rochester city schools still remain challenged in finding a good formula that will keep more young people in school and programs that will prepare them for the needs of a different non-manufacturing world.

Everywhere in Rochester you see the marks left behind by George Eastman's philanthropy: the Eastman Dental Clinic; Eastman Theater, home of the Rochester

Philharmonic which he supported generously; the George Eastman House, the home that he occupied until his death and which in later years became an outstanding museum of photography.

You couldn't ask for more culture than Rochester has to offer with a world class symphony orchestra and a theater company that annually produces a number of significant performances. Rochester is the home of Garth Fagan, whose choreography of *Lion King* won major awards. Many people know the flugelhorn music of Grammy winner Chuck Mangione, a Rochesterian and Eastman School of Music graduate. The art world has been awed by the steel sculptings of artist Albert Paley that range from table pieces to eight-story building-height works of art.

When it comes to homes, you can find everything from the small closely spaced houses of the city to stately mansions on Rochester's East Avenue and in the city's suburbs. Small homes surround the massive 1100 acre Kodak Park, the former center of Kodak manufacturing now renamed Eastman Business Park. In other areas were homes for Italian tailors who came to work in the famous Rochester clothing factories. Other areas served as neighborhood centers for Irish, Germans, Poles and many other ethnic groups.

Today the suburbs of Rochester sport million dollar houses with their vast lawns and unique architecture, like the famous Mushroom House built on stilts. Other stately homes dot the shorelines of the nearby Finger Lakes.

Rochester's downtown has suffered, as have the centers of many cities in America. Suburban malls in the area continue to grow and prosper with leading store chains from around the country operating profitably in Rochester.

If you are building your business in a digital world, your likely choices of locations would be California's Silicon Valley, the Route 128 corridor north of Boston, or now possibly Austin, Texas or one of the sunny cities in Florida. The infrastructure for the digital world never fully reached Rochester and even today the development of several incubator sites only offers a small window into the world of tomorrow that will consist of silicon, bio and nano technologies.

What does the future of Rochester hold? Well, for one thing Rochester offers all-year sports, professional, college, and enthusiastic high school programs. In addition to soccer, lacrosse and hockey teams, Rochester has a baseball stadium only a few years old, new soccer stadium, and an arena that not only provides great ice hockey but also a show venue for visiting ice shows, circuses, and more. Ski slopes are less than an hour's drive from the city.

A renewed downtown Rochester will bring new life to the center of Rochester. The old Erie Canal has proved to be a drawing card for both day trips and for various activities along its shores. Major projects are under way to enhance the canal and offer more attractions.

Few people realize that practically within the city borders grapes are grown and wine is pressed into some of the varietals that consistently win awards. Just south of Rochester, hills of cultured grapes can be seen with varietals that have won international recognition. A few miles to the east of Rochester, on the Seneca Indian reservation, a major gambling casino can take your money as can a new casino in Niagara Falls, just one hour to the west.

Rochester has been the butt of many jokes about the local weather. But Rochester is a great place for families to grow and businesses to prosper.

For almost 100 years Kodak was the place to work if you lived in Rochester, a city of just over a million people. Fathers, mothers, sons and daughters, and grandchildren—yes, families had great pride in being Kodak families. Kodak was a male bastion until World War II where employees worked for a lifetime for the company. It was often joked that Kodak people had yellow blood (like the color of the Kodak packaging) because they were so loyal to their company.

Rochester was never quite a Kodak company town, but it was likely that your neighbor once worked for Kodak, your fellow church goers were Kodakers and your world was centered in Rochester. There are many people who believe that this may have been a factor in Kodak's slow move to electronic and digital photography; Rochester people did not realize the impact of the changing world, and they were too sheltered by the Kodak of the past.

Kodak did a lot for its employees. Until late in the last century, at both Kodak Office and Kodak Park, employees could enjoy a portion of a feature film each day in an employee auditorium. These major movies were representative of Kodak's film product in use so they were considered a good investment for employee pride.

Kodak had a very active camera club and other social groups as well. Today the Kodak Camera Club and the darkrooms are closed.

There were many other Kodak social events as well. For example, there was a special annual award given to 25-year employees, which also involved dinner with senior management.   Until recent years, it was not unusual to see Kodak employees celebrating 40 or 45 years of service. Today it is challenging to keep employees for any length of time at Kodak because of the changing programs and the constant need for downsizing. Consequently, employment for the future is always questionable to potential new employees.

Then there was the store for employees where Kodak film, cameras and other photographic accessories could be purchased at reduced prices. This store never seemed to create competition for local businesses, but knowing that a large part of the community was not purchasing products from outside dealers was always an underlying thought.

A few years ago, Xerox, another major Rochester employer, moved its corporate headquarters to Connecticut to bring it closer to the New York City financial center. This move has been watched carefully by Kodak watchers. The move of Kodak's Consumer Products Division to Atlanta in 2000 seemed to be an indication that Rochester might not be the ideal place for a company headquarters.

Rumors about moving Kodak's Rochester headquarters have circulated for several years, but it has not happened. Some of the Kodak buildings around the Tower headquarters have been sold and others carry "For Sale" signs or have been sold, but the Kodak Tower still stands on State Street.

Every spring, from 1918 to 1992, when the famous Kodak annual bonus was paid, people lined up at automobile showrooms to buy their new cars and appliance stores to buy their refrigerators, stoves and other luxuries. Today, Kodak pays its employees for performance, but it is not the umbrella set up by George Eastman almost 100 years ago. The company was no longer ready for the next downsizing that would affect the greatly reduced staff of Kodak in Rochester.

Sadly, the vision of many people who worked at Kodak both in high positions and lowly factory positions was not a global vision. Everything revolved about Rochester, everything related to photography came in a yellow box and traditional film was the king because it was highly profitable as were most of the products manufactured at Kodak Park with its sprawling network of roads, railroads, and interconnected utilities.

Kodak went from being the largest employer in Rochester with over 60,000 local employees four decades ago to 5,100 now and still shrinking. Today, the largest employer is the University of Rochester along with its Medical Center and other facilities.

Kodak manufacturing and research jobs have disappeared and have been replaced by many new entrepreneurial companies that have opened in Rochester. It is the reinvention of an entire community and area.

Kodak Employees in Rochester, NY

Year	Employees
1982	60,400
1985	54,200
1990	42,200
1995	34,000
2000	23,900
2005	14,100
2010	7,400
2011	5,100

Source: Rochester Business Journal

By the end of the 1980's, all of the entrepreneurial or Kodak-acquired companies had been shelved. In large companies like Kodak, entrepreneurial companies are difficult to manage and take a great deal of management time. Independent entrepreneurial companies offer far greater rewards than can be offered inside a large corporation like Kodak.

Downsizing after downsizing had sapped away many experienced people at Kodak. The story of one of more than a dozen downsizings may give an insight into the challenge of not only constructing the program for a downsizing but also the sensitivities of people involved in constructing these downsizings.

At the beginning of the '90s, it was felt that another downsizing was needed to improve Kodak's bottom line. There was a planning session held just prior to what was to be a disastrous quarterly report.

At that time Kodak had been through half a dozen downsizings and it was becoming painful to both employees and management. Senior managers at the meeting were trying to do the impossible by having one major layoff instead of the continual series of layoffs. It was finally decided that 1800 would be a good number, but before things were completed, the number increased to 3400 and because of the need to meet legal rights issues, the pool worldwide of eligible workers was 8,800.

Because the package was so good, 8,400 took it and Kodak manufacturing suffered because of the loss of many skilled people. It is often said that film and paper manufacturing may be 95% science, but some think it is 5% witchcraft. Actually the 5% comes from skilled employees, many with 25 or more years of experience in film and paper manufacturing; these were the people who left.

While not digital, it seems that the Kodak headquarters in Rochester had considered taking out a license for a television station in Rochester when the first TV stations were being built in the '50s. The first license in Rochester went to WHAM that started on Channel 6 and later moved to Channel 8 because of interference with Syracuse. Kodak was supposed to partner with Dumont, both were image related businesses. Perhaps this would've made a difference in how Kodak people looked at electronics.

Chapter Two—The Instant Mistake

Kodak did it right when it introduced the line of Kodak Instamatic film cameras in 1963. At that time, one of the biggest problems that consumers usually encountered with 35mm cameras was loading the film. How many unhappy vacationers came back with no pictures because the film wasn't put in the camera correctly? The answer to the problem was the Instamatic cartridge-loading camera. More than 50 million of these cameras were produced by 1970.

Some people today still remember the original commercials for the Instamatic camera in which a parachutist loaded, while falling, a cartridge into an Instamatic camera. As a follow-up to the original Instamatic, Kodak brought out the smaller sized pocket Instamatic and a new 110 film cartridge. Twenty-five million of these cameras were sold in slightly over three years. The pocket Instamatic was a greater challenge because of the smaller size film and the challenge of getting the same quality prints as were produced by the original Instamatic.

The pocket Instamatic also brought one of the first of a number of lawsuits against Eastman Kodak Company for antitrust. The Berkey case was based on the fact that Kodak had not disclosed information to other manufacturers about their new 110 system. Berkey ultimately lost the trial, but this also stimulated GAF Corporation into filing an antitrust suit against Kodak. Kodak looked like an easy target to GAF Chairman Dr. Jesse Werner, who seemed to have a dislike for Kodak Chairman Dr. Louis Eilers.

Kodak kept a litigation office open for a decade. Kodak had a big legal database--it was needed.

Back in 1947, Edwin Land demonstrated a new camera that produced black-and-white images that developed in a minute from the time they were pulled from his camera. Land had tried to sell his original idea of black-and-white instant photography to Kodak. But until the mid-'80s, Kodak's management was worried about antitrust, that the company would get in trouble with the government. That attitude took a lot of energy instead of directing their thoughts and their ideas on where they should have been going.

Louis Eilers Kodak CEO
1970-1977

When the Polaroid color camera arrived in the early 1960s it produced revenue for Kodak because the color sensitized material for the camera was coated by Kodak

Edwin Land Polaroid CEO
1937-1980

until 1969, but Land was taking his coating business elsewhere. Apparently Kodak Chairman Dr. Eilers, whose background was chemistry like many of the other CEOs who preceded him at Kodak, didn't like Edwin Land because he felt that Land didn't appreciate how much Kodak had done to help develop Land's product.

Kodak wanted to continue to receive the income for coating the Polaroid peel-apart color material. So Dr. Eilers decided, in the late 1960s, to develop a product like the Polaroid color material and Kodak Research Labs (KRL) conducted research until 1972 when Polaroid surprised Kodak with the announcement of a new SX-70 camera with a new color film that no longer required the peel-apart process. Kodak had suspected that Polaroid had an integral product coming but didn't know when it would appear in the market.

So Kodak was developing their two instant products in parallel, one was the color peel-apart product (P-129) and the other the integral product (P-130). You had to wonder if the effort to develop a competitive product was revenge or because of a profit motive—an unproved or adequately analyzed profit motive. When Kodak patent attorneys reported to Eilers their concern over patented rollers used in the Polaroid integrated product, Eilers who was known for his temper, told them, "Let the bastards sue us."

Kodak dropped the peel-apart process research and immediately started working on its own process for creating instant color prints with no customer handling. The biggest challenge was to avoid a head-on collision with Polaroid patents.

But now a new CEO, Walter Fallon, was leading the charge to develop a competitor for Polaroid's single pack color product and he took a personal interest. Kodak learned a great deal that would serve other purposes during the development of the instant color product. The Kodak instant dye releasers used for instant photography later became dye releasers for Kodak Ektaflex and later for Fuji Pictography that Fujifilm licensed from Kodak.

The P-130 project was run by a project manager who had a number of people working for him in a matrix management approach. The researcher's individual manager would not know what they were doing—security was important.

The group had no instant cameras so the test products would be put in a 4 x 5-inch camera back and pictures taken. In the darkroom they had rollers that would roll on the cover sheet and develop the pictures. They would work all weekend and Fallon would do a review the following Monday.

Fallon became known to the people who worked on the instant project as the "800 Pound Gorilla". It was said he was teaching the elephant to dance. But Fallon was the chemist with no marketing training or experience. The elephant never danced on Fallon's watch. There were times when he absolutely tore apart people making presentations. If he didn't like the design of a camera he would sweep it off the table and tell the people who designed and built it to "Go back to work, guys."

If you were straight with Walter Fallon he accepted what you said, but many people were afraid of him and told him what he wanted to hear. They would say they had experiments under way to solve problems and they didn't. It's hard for a guy on top to know what is real or if people are parroting what he wanted to hear. Fallon was too involved with the details of projects. He wasn't a man of vision who could handle all the details.

The people in research would develop new coatings and when they got a good one, they had the capability of making some experimental picture units that they could use in some really primitive cameras. They'd go on a field trip. One of their favorites would be to go to Palm Springs, California, where it was warm; it would be in the middle of winter in Rochester.

The packages that researchers had developed in Rochester worked very well in the lab. In one case, they were shooting in a desert environment and the black layers in the film were black gooey. They performed great at 105° but what they didn't realize was that the back heated up to over 200° in the pack, they didn't work. So it was back to the drawing boards. It was a tough process but Kodak researchers were world class and handled it well.

As a system, instant wasn't as good as people thought it was. Instant wasn't going anywhere; it had some applications and from a marketing point of view, Kodak tried to add some pizzazz to it, but the cameras were too bulky and the pictures were not that good—neither Kodak's nor Polaroid's.

Kodak EK4 Instant Camera

Kodak launched its line of color instant cameras in April of 1976 and by the end of the month, on April 26, 1976, Polaroid Corporation had legally filed a complaint charging that Eastman Kodak Company had infringed 12 Polaroid patents relating to integral instant cameras and film for which they were asking $12 billion.

The next five years were years of legal discovery with Kodak having the advantage of previously collected records relating to both the Berkey and GAF lawsuits at the time of the launch of the Kodak Instamatic cameras, but it was still a tedious process.

There was one problem in the discovery process. One of Kodak's outside law firm partners had forgotten to turn over a box of documents to Polaroid. While the box contained no documents of value, the judge was furious and many people suspected that if there was any possibility of Kodak winning the lawsuit, they were then doomed. Kodak later sued the law firm and recover damages but the damages were a pittance compared to the final settlement.

In October of 1981, Judge Rya Zobel, in her Boston courtroom, listened to witness after witness for four and a half months.

In September 1985 in a carefully worded document, Judge Zobel found that Kodak had infringed on 20 claims of seven valid Polaroid patents. In addition, she found two patents were invalid and one not infringed. One patent was found invalid before the trial and Polaroid withdrew its claims on another patent as well.

The Polaroid settlement from Judge Zobel was $5.7 billion but was finally settled for $995 million. In the meantime, Kodak stopped manufacturing cameras and film. In her final award, October 12, 1990, Judge Zobel indicated that while Kodak had infringed patents, it was not willful or deliberate.

There were additional costs beyond the judge's settlement. Kodak had built, at Fallon's direction, thirteen $1 million packaging machines to pack the new instant film product. People involved in the project felt that one machine was all that was needed so in the end, all 13 machines were destroyed. It was another example of the lack of good market planning.

In some ways it was ironic that all of this had occurred. Actually Kodak was in many ways anxious to get out of the instant business which did not prove to be as successful and profitable as they thought it would be. Kodak left the instant camera business in January 1986. Before Kodak could announce a voluntary program to compensate owners of instant cameras, a class action suit was filed against Kodak and finally settled in 1988.

The "Instant" debacle was another of the early ill-formed CEO interventions that ultimately led to Kodak's bankruptcy—it was one of the pieces that many saw as a mystery when a well-founded and successful company falls into challenging times. There have been a lot of these in recent years. It was a slow and near death experience.

The strange twist was that Polaroid filed for bankruptcy in 2001 and stopped the manufacture of instant film at the end of 2008. A decade later, Kodak followed the same path to bankruptcy.

A patent gives an inventor or whoever is assigned the patent, exclusive rights for a limited period of time in exchange for public disclosure of the invention. Kodak did not patent every development because it would give information away. An example by another company gives some explanation to the concept of "Not filing". Gold sensitization of film emulsions was done by Ansco in the 1930s to increase black-and-white film speeds. It took Kodak several years of research to understand the concept because no patents were ever filed on the technique.

A patent can be a great protection for "Intellectual property" or it can give a false sense of security that either a product or concept is not infringing another's patent, but it is no protection from the need for litigation.

Some thought that film would live forever. Unfortunately, there were far too many filmcentric people at Kodak who could not think in their wildest imagination that anything would replace film.

Kodak, in their manufacturing processes, used digital image processing in the mid-'70s to determine the performance of new film products being built. Digital was alive at Kodak and even had begun to fabricate imaging sensors in a small way.

In a small back room of Kodak's largest equipment manufacturing site called Elmgrove, a young graduate electronic engineer, Steve Sasson, was given his first project, "Make us a digital camera." Just out of college, Steve was familiar with the early CCD imagers; they had been invented at the famous Bell Labs a decade before. He was able to get a 100 x 100 pixel imager from Fairchild.

He looked in a scrap box in the film movie camera department and found a lens. To record the **Steve Sasson Digital Camera** information from the sensor, he fed the output to a cassette recorder. The package was a little larger than a portable typewriter case. Steve had made a digital camera that could capture black-and-white images.

A patent was filed in 1976 setting the origin date for the first digital camera. He lugged that ugly gadget around Kodak and took pictures, but everywhere he went he was told, "Forget it, don't bother us."

To give Kodak the credit for inventing the digital camera, two decades after the initial digital camera patent was filed; Sasson was paraded around the world as the inventor of the digital camera and was even honored at the White House with the National Medal of Technology and Innovation. All of this attention certainly did not make up for the neglect that had been given to Steve Sasson and digital photography by Kodak over the same quarter century.

The 1981announcement of Sony's Mavica got Kodak management attention. There were some 82 Kodak acquisitions after the Sony Mavica announcement. We'll talk more about that in the next chapter. These acquisitions covered everything from snow-making machines to magnetic media where the magnetic coating material was mixed in California and shipped for coating to Rochester, but magnetic properties changed when shipped that far—at least that is the story being told.

There wasn't one acquisition or venture standing five years later. Some could see that their cash cow film could be affected. Sony's president, Akio Morita, was quoted as saying that Sony would become "the Kodak of electronic photography." The gauntlet had been thrown in front of Kodak electronically. Digital photography would follow in less than a decade.

One thing Kodak tried to do was develop a strategy for those markets that would really be film-oriented like in developing countries and focus more on digital in the developed markets and manage both. Some thought that you couldn't do both—you couldn't manage a digital initiative simultaneously with film initiative without one sabotaging the other.

Dr. John P. White joined Kodak in 1988 after Kodak acquired the California company he headed, Interactive Systems. As General Manager of the Integration and Systems Products Division, he was to put digital on track for Kodak. He left in 1992, just before the arrival of Dr. George Fisher. When he looked around Kodak, he saw a lot of innovative products but Kodak was unable to bring them together into attractive marketing packages. White had good vision but left Kodak with no additional markers on the road to a digital Kodak, it was still a film culture.

Some Kodak Acquisitions

Spin Physics: acquired in 1972, it became part of the Mass Memory Division. It served two segments of the electronics market with magnetic products: 1) high performance magnetic recording heads and 2) high speed video motion analysis systems. Located in San Diego, CA.

Atex: acquired in 1981, was a business unit within the Commercial and Information Systems organization but now closed. It addressed the text-processing needs of the publishing industry. Located in Bedford, MA.

Datatape: acquired in 1983 from Bell & Howell, it was part of Government Systems Division. Makers of specialty magnetic data recorders, such as those used in the space shuttle. Located in Pasadena, CA.

Diconix: acquired from Mead in 1983, was a business unit of the Commercial and Information Systems group. Manufactured inkjet printers for use in the office and personal computer markets. In the late 1980s, became Kodak's Dayton Operations where the Kodak Prosper Stream Inkjet Press was designed and built. Located in Dayton, OH.

Eikonix: acquired in May 1985, was a business unit of the Commercial and Information Systems Division, now closed. Research, design and manufacture digital image processing equipment and computer-aided electro-optical systems, merged with Atex in 1986. Located in Bedford, MA.

Verbatim: acquired via tender in May 1985. Maker of flexible magnetic media for personal computers. Purchased by Kodak in 1984 for $174 million and sold in 1990 to

Mitsubishi Chemical Corp. for $200 million. Located in Sunnyvale, CA.

Garlic Technology Corp. (GTC): acquired majority of assets in July 1985. Specialists in design and development of advanced digital magnetic recording heads. Kodak was to establish an advanced development center for digital recording head design: Garlic Development Corporation. Based in Morgan Hill, CA.

Xertronix, Inc.: acquired in August 1985. Products included equipment to clean semiconductor wafers, memory disks, and masking plates. Chief product: top load double cassette rinser/dryer. Based in Rochester, NY.

Oce-Skycopy Ltd.: acquired by Kodak Limited in August 1985. Was a distributor of graphic arts products in the United Kingdom. Based in London.

Pacific Film Laboratories: Largest photographic processing and retailing operation in Australia. Purchased for undisclosed amount by Kodak Australasia on 11/13/85.

Kusuda: announced 11/13/85, Kodak acquired three units of Kusuda Business Machines Co.: 1) the Division for Kodak Products, 2) The Kusuda Microsystems Services Company, and 3) Nippon Information Publishing Company. Acquisitions made for undisclosed sum. Purpose: to directly market, service, and distribute Kodak micrographics and business imaging systems products in Japan. Based in Osaka, Japan.

Consolidated Magnetics Corporation (CMC): acquired by Datatape subsidiary on 12/4/85 for undisclosed amount of cash. Manufacturer of magnetic head components used in rotary magnetic tape recorders. Based in Santa Clara, CA.

Cyclotomics: acquired 12/20/85 for undisclosed amount of cash. A leading developer of digital error detection and correction systems. Based in Berkeley, CA.

BASO Precision Optics: acquired capital stock on 1/2/86. A maker of precision optical elements for a variety of applications. Terms of agreement not announced. Based in Taichung, Taiwan.

Chapter Three—The 800 Pound Gorilla

Walter Fallon was appointed CEO in 1973. Gerald Zornow, Kodak's Chairman who was making $330,000 a year at the time could not conceive how any person could be worth over $1000 a day for any company. Fallon wanted $450,000, so the Kodak Board gave him that and they raised Zornow to $600,000 almost doubling his pay.

Walter Fallon Kodak CEO 1977-1983

Today, you can't find a chairman, president or CEO who will work for those wages. Fallon became personally involved in many development projects. He was nicknamed the "800 pound gorilla." He was somewhat of a bully at times, a figure to be reckoned with. He was a very strong-willed and autocratic kind of person, much like Edwin Land, whose inventions built Polaroid. If you talk to people who knew Land, you get some of the same reactions as Fallon got at Kodak.

Fallon had some idiosyncrasies that may have come from his years of growing up in Kodak. When Fallon was expected to fly on the company airplane, the maintenance staff had to quickly install a partition in the airplane to give Fallon a private compartment.

He had always wanted an executive dining room for the senior officers of the company. Finally one was constructed adjacent to the cafeteria at Kodak's main offices. When it came time to select the furniture for the new executive dining room, Fallon personally picked out the tables. They were standard tables found in every high school in the United States.

It was a real class act. Managers did not like to use the executive dining room because they thought it was helpful to have lunch with the employees as a way of hearing what was going on and maintaining better communications.

The work-in-progress that you could find within Kodak was amazing. In 1979 and 1980 Kodak was developing digital cameras for the Department of Defense. By 1981, the camera quality was good enough to read license plates on cars. It was a decade later that Kodak showed a digital camera designed for professionals at the 1990 Photokina in Cologne, Germany.

Those same Kodak government design people who did the imaginative camera designs and other projects for the government had a hand in designing Kodak's black-and-white copier. Far better than what Xerox was offering at the time, it was built to stand up under hard use and produce outstanding image quality.

Fallon did not like copiers because of the financial exposure caused by a large lease program since Kodak would own all the leased machines. If the program failed, Kodak would have a big write-off. Fallon had other games to play; copiers never got the attention the product line deserved. Xerox was relieved.

It was obvious that Fallon had limited knowledge of products that Kodak might offer. Film and color photo paper, with their profit margins reaching 65 to 75%, were, of course, more attractive. But the future growth of copiers would open new opportunities for Kodak in long-term leases and the sale of toners, papers, and services.

Kodak once before had a copy product called Verifax. Kodak Verifax copier products had been made obsolete when Xerox appeared in the marketplace.

It was a long, bitterly contested time for Kodak. While Kodak was immersed in the Polaroid patent litigation, development was under way for a new concept in cameras that was launched in 1982. The Kodak (film) Disc camera proved to be another misstep for Kodak.

The Disc camera was supposed to be Kodak Chairman Walter Fallon's last hurrah, but Kodak technical people tried valiantly to delay the introduction because the very small Disc film images on production film did not live up to the quality of images made during the camera's initial tests.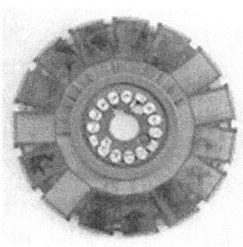

Kodak Disc Film

They needed another year to develop a new film that would provide a higher quality image, but nothing was going to slow Fallon's child.

Anyone who spoke out against the disc camera the matter what their level of management, they could expect a "chewing out". It was suggested to one senior Kodak executive who did not like the results from trying the disc camera before introduction that the individual taking the pictures had some chemical substance that affected the film result. Kodak researchers were grasping for straws.

Because of the unique size and shape of the Disc, new processing and printing equipment was required by finishers, a decision that finishers would soon regret because of the short life of the whole Disc system. Less than half a dozen years after the Disc introduction, all production was stopped. Kodak had been trapped by significant improvements in both the easy loading and quality of 35mm cameras. Kodak began producing 35mm cameras again with models in the same price range as Disc cameras.

One bright spot occurred with Disc camera in Cologne, Germany, at the bi-annual Photokina show. Kodak had been quietly developing CCD sensor technology in their research laboratories and used that technology to create a video player for Disc film. The player was demonstrated to the public at the 1982 Photokina when the Kodak Disc camera was introduced. It was interesting to watch the major Japanese manufacturers look with surprise at the good quality of the large-screen images that were produced from Disc film.

What Photokina visitors did not know was that Kodak had hastily put together the Disc film show imager. It was a one-of-a-kind unit that required serious nightly maintenance to keep it running and producing the images people were seeing. You would sometimes think that the system was held together with chewing gum and hairpins. You might not have been too far off the mark.

Possibly because of the Disc-to-video player, rumors spread in Japan that Kodak was planning to laser-print Disc images. That was a possibility since one solution developed by Kodak Research for significantly improving the printing quality was to digitally scan print the Disc films, a process that had been around Kodak for several years, but had never been commercialized. Kodak had many concepts that never made it to saleable products.

Sample digital prints were made and Kodak people who saw them liked the quality. However, it was a technique for printing consumer images that didn't occur in general usage until many years later. Because it meant an increase of one to two cents in the cost per print, the idea was rejected and it was almost two decades later before the concept became universally adopted, mostly by Kodak competitors.

Another solution was proposed for making sharper prints from Disc film. Kodak manufacturing had put a 'a roughness or tooth' on the back side of Disc film to help a static problem, but it did result in a loss of sharpness.

Apparently the easy solution was to coat the Disc film with a 3M product called Photoguard. The solution worked for reducing static, but there was another lawsuit standing in the way because Kodak had sued 3M for infringing with the Photoguard product on a lacquer that was put on Kodak's Kodachrome film. CEO Fallon made the decision not to use a 3M product that was involved in a Kodak-initiated patent litigation. You had to wonder if it was the role of the CEO to be so heavily involved in simple decisions.

Kodak Disc cameras looked amazingly like today's pocketable digital cameras. The only problem was that the Disc did not live up to the quality expectations of the customers of that period who were used to prints from 35mm film. Disc film and cameras disappeared in a short time. Kodak had another failure to contend with; they were beginning to add up.

There was a sense that there was a finite life for film and the idea was to be able to maximize the role, the brand, the channel, and be the last one standing in the health sciences field. Kodak was highly respected in the medical and dental communities because of the quality of the x-ray products but Kodak had developed. The company would want to acquire several other companies which products fitted well into a health services market.

Radiology departments and the radiologists were Kodak's very close contacts for many years. They were originally the decision makers on purchasing radiology supplies but now they had to share the decision-making with hospital administration. Ultimately the decisions for all departments became administrative issues and the long-term relationships that had been built were less meaningful. No longer would the free 35mm film work as a way of gaining entry to a hospital or radiology department.

Anticipating changes in the medical records field, Kodak had an ill-timed microfilm product, the Retinar System that lasted less than a year. The product, designed for Radiology departments, was a new radiology image storage system that Fallon supported. The Retinar product came from Kodak's Recordak experience with microfilm. Retinar reduced large film x-rays to small film images on a card that could be read with a projector. It was not a digital solution but it was intended to reduce the need for storing large x-ray films.

Strangely, it was not the cost of the system (estimated to be $50,000), or the image quality (concern for artifacts) that killed Retinar. It was the AMA's concern for patient privacy that stopped the project. Six systems were built; one system was sold and shipped then repurchased and returned to Kodak. One unit was damaged in a shipping accident and the other four were scrapped—complex optical systems were all destroyed.

Retinar was a good idea, but again, Kodak people had an answer but had not asked the customers the needed questions first. This ended an early attempt at upgrading hospital records that would be done in the future digitally. Kodak had another product failure.

A word that you heard too often used to describe Kodak managers was arrogant. The arrogance appeared when looking at new concepts, dealing with potential new competitors, or dealing with common service people outside of Kodak. Arrogance appeared far too often in Kodak's business dealings.

One senior manager, who apparently was not flying on one of the Kodak airplanes during a United Airlines strike, had a problem with his commercial flight. The UA agent who was helping him tried to provide alternatives for his cancelled flight. He didn't like the flight she provided and actually brought the woman agent to tears. You had to wonder what it was like to work for this manager.

Kodavision 8mm Video Camera

Kodak established an electronic division in the 1980s and Dan Carp headed this early organization. Later, Carp would be the 1988 Kodak candidate for the MIT Sloan School-- the path through which many Kodak future CEOs traveled.

The first electronic product was another short-lived product that offered new opportunities for Kodak that never happened. It was the Kodavision Series 2000 8mm video system and video cassettes were introduced at the same time. Part of the story was told to me by the man who negotiated it with Panasonic.

Negotiations included a meeting with Konosuke Matsushita, the founder of the company and a very significant and admired figure in Japanese industry. It was like meeting an Emperor—he actually came in his formal Japanese robes to the meeting and gave his blessing to the Kodak 8mm video product. Panasonic even expressed interest in having Kodak distribute Panasonic products. But that never happened.

Entry into the market was almost as fast as its exit a year later. The sudden exit was to haunt Kodak in future years. It was difficult to create relationships with Japanese companies because many in Japan felt that Kodak could not be depended upon to last through the evolvement of a new product.

The cameras didn't sell; there was no marketing money. It takes a certain time for the market to develop and for people to receive the product and all of these things just didn't have time to happen. Kodak needed to manage the cost in a way that they could have at least a breakeven business initially, but the film people in charge did not allow that to happen.

The product was out of Kodak in a year. Rumors were that the Kodak sale had not been approved by Matsushitasan--a good rumor to cover inept marketing in an unfamiliar product area. The real fact was that nobody in Kodak in Rochester wanted to sell it or fund it. Kodak was a film company--film ruled the day. Another electronic product opportunity was lost.

In 1980, Kodak was telling its customers don't worry about the changes in electronics, "When the time is right we'll be there." That was the company's marketing slogan in the '80s. But customers were saying; we don't want to be left with somebody that is not keeping up. We are willing to stay with you, Kodak, but if you're not preparing, we'll find someone else. For the future, Kodak was nervous about staying. When the time is right, Kodak will be there, Kodak kept saying. But what was the right time?

The difference between Kodak and Japanese philosophies are comparable to baseball with the Japanese batting a lot more singles and Kodak only aiming for and wanting a home run each time they were at bat.

Kodak manufactured imaging sensors not only for Kodak projects but for other manufacturers' applications. Kodak forgot its great heritage and base of knowledge about what was needed to make a good photograph. If they kept their sensor development small, and expensive, maybe it would go away, or so some had hoped.

Fujifilm, as a competitive film company, took Kodak's attention more than any other competitor, and there were not too many in the film world. Fuji, in the future, will probably be the surviving supplier because they have a long-term vision and did things at the beginning that will be far-reaching.

For example, Fuji knew that digital technology was going to be part of the future so they formed a design team and they developed expertise in the design of semi-conductor sensors. In 1991 Fuji built a factory of their own to make sensors and cameras. They did not go out and buy sensors; they were in the position of actually designing and building all their own sensors. The design control over the sensor was critical. They spoke of it early as the camera equivalent of film and, of course, it was.

Fuji operated with very lean staffs. As an example, their public relations department in the US had less than five people to Kodak's 50 or so. Fuji licensed every patent that Kodak offered. A successful Fuji photo product, Pictrography, used for thermal color photo digital printing was Kodak-licensed technology.

Rochester people thought that Kodak color images were perfect because they were so natural. Fuji came along with color negative films that produce bright blue skies and bright colors. Finally, Kodak went to customers and asked them what they like; they found out that what Fuji was providing in imaging was what the customers actually wanted.

When Kodak people went to Japan, they were told that "Kodak's key mission for Kodak people visiting Japan was to make trouble for Fuji." Ultimately, Kodak had a research center and offices in Japan but closed them a decade after opening them, it was too expensive having Rochester research labs and other labs in Japan and Europe.

When digital came along, almost at the time of the invention of CCD and CMOS imagers, the decision-makers at Kodak found digital interesting but were sure in their minds that it would never equal silver halide. It was a strange situation but Kodak had good scientists who had great vision but were always blinded by the extreme profitability of film. The worst thing was that they were the victims of their own success.

In 1990, Kodak's Professional Division showed a prototype of a megapixel digital camera design for professional applications. A year later, Kodak marketed a digital camera for the press and also a special model for Associated Press (AP). Priced at about $17,000, it marked the beginning of a new style of photo journalism that would affect the pictures in our newspapers and magazines. It reminded you of the early burdensome cameras for photography news work of over 100 years ago.

The first consumer digital camera Kodak produced was made for Apple and called the Apple QuickTake 100, released in 1994. Kodak's goal for the camera was to be as good as storage cards that were available then, but the Quicktake camera used a direct connect to the computer and a non-standard image forrmat that required translation.

The work that Kodak had done on the QuickTake camera led to some serious discussions between Kodak and Apple about the possibility of Kodak buying Apple. But the negotiations broke off a few months after they started in 1992.

Myopic vision was one of the greatest problems that faced Kodak over the years. It was difficult and even challenging to get people to look outside of the comfort of film and its associated products. Profit margins were beyond belief, 65 to 75%, and the rare was the manager who would believe that anything might disrupt that comfortable business. The Kodak brand had worldwide recognition and Kodak cameras were the memory makers of the world. Would anyone believe that within two decades, Kodak would begin to fall and enter bankruptcy in one additional decade. Kodak's sole defense was film.

Chapter Four—The Common Man's Chief

Kay Whitmore and Colby Chandler had imperial chairmanships and were definitely not accessible. Both were engineers at Kodak Park and each had received a Sloan Fellowship at MIT. Chandler was known for driving his own pickup truck to work each day and parking in the executive garage. He was friendly and approachable in social situations but not easily reached in his tower office.

Colby Chandler Kodak CEO 1983-1990

Chandler chose as his president Kay Whitmore and J. Phillip Samper, another Sloan-MIT graduate worked closely with Chandler and Whitmore who had chemistry backgrounds and Samper was trained in business in California.

Samper had recognized the changing direction to digital in many areas of business—Kodak business. He was the continuous champion of the need for change at Kodak.

It was becoming apparent that Kodak employees had grown complacent. People could look around and see that performance was not related to advancement and that many people in Kodak had lost their work ethic—the thing that made Kodak a successful company.

A company officer one morning visited one of Kodak's several cafeterias after the time of normal beginning of business hours and found it filled with people having breakfast. He raised many eyebrows when he asked the cafeteria manager to close the cafeteria at 8 AM and let people know that they should have breakfast at home.

In an all-employee meeting broadcast To All Offices and Presented at the Kodak Park Auditorium he told Kodak people that Kodak professionals who are doing their job by working eight – five, they were mistaken. Sadly, he received some serious hate mail because of the talk. Kodak Rochester people were not ready to do what was necessary to make Kodak digitally competitive.

Kodak was now in a competitive race for its film business and even more so in the electronic and digital imaging areas that were about to unfold.

Since early 1980s, Kodak management had been downsizing the company's assets and work force, but not its airplane fleet. At one time a company plane was the one of the first thing to go when companies found themselves with need to downsize. Strangely, Kodak acquired more planes. According to management, the Kodak planes offered a very valuable service.

"Only with distinctive cultural changes could Kodak again be identified as the imaging leader. It will take more than high-speed copiers and high-definition television conversion devices to earn the respect of both employees and the world market of customers and investors."(Commentary by John Larish in the Rochester Democrat & Chronicle, 11/12/89)

A month before I retired from Kodak, my last presentation in December 1983 was to Colby Chandler, Kay Whitmore and J. Philip Samper, the three men who in 1986 would form the Office of the Chief Executive, a unique experiment in running Kodak. Chandler would be Chairman and CEO, Samper Vice Chairman and Whitmore President. It would be a troika with all three men side by side just as they were at this moment.

In my presentation, I shared my several years of observations of the growing impact of consumer electronics and made a recommendation that Kodak hire an executive from the electronics industry to head that function. Both the Chandler and Samper took notes, but the president and future CEO of Kodak Whitmore slept through the presentation.

My boss, Vince Barabba, Kodak's Director of Market Intelligence, and Samper continued to try to get the message of the digital future across at Kodak. Their analysis indicated that digital imaging technologies would begin to predominate at the end of the 1990s. You had to wonder if they knew about digital high resolution work Kodak had been doing for the Federal government that might have strengthened their case with the filmcentrics of Kodak. Barabba left Kodak in 1985.

A few months later, I attended a trade event in Chicago and was sitting in the front row. Right behind me was Bill Gates of Microsoft. I'd heard that he was in Rochester the week before so I turned around and asked him, "How did you like the weather in Rochester?" Rochester was known for its 18% gray skies.

I didn't get an answer from Bill, only a grunt sound and a shake of his head. I later learned that Kay Whitmore had fallen asleep during a meeting with Bill. Whitmore suffered from a thyroid condition that caused him to fall asleep easily. No one knew about it and even when the condition was later corrected with surgery, no public information was released.

A year or so later, I had a chance to have a one-on-one conversation with Bill Gates and discovered he was one of the most pleasant people I've ever interviewed. No mention was made of his earlier Rochester visit.

Unknown to most people, other Kodak studies of where the electronic industry was going were being conducted, but it was an example of the uncoordinated efforts that certainly was not going to bring Kodak easily or successfully into the New Age it would face in the next decade.

Kodak may have gone off track because things ascribed to major customers may at times have been presented as facts were actually questionable. At major management meetings, a senior manager might announce that customer XYZ insisted on some new business or product needs.

Many times these needs or products were solely the managers' idea and it was their way of selling it. The customer knew nothing about it. It was not unusual for a customer to receive a call after a meeting in which the customer's name was used and the customer sold on the idea that he needed the product or service that had been ascribed to him. You might think of this as reverse customer intelligence, but a risky strategy that often resulted in a loss of focus in real customer needs.

Several people who were responsible for information and information collection at Kodak complained that their materials were conveniently modified at each management layer as the information made its way to the Kodak Board of Directors. While each management step had the right of editorial review and editing, changing factual data seemed to be risky and may have contributed to Kodak's delayed response to the changing times. While some data collectors stood by their numbers, others said changes were made to meet changing conditions—whatever those might be. Decisions needed to be made but there would be a good chance that that the massaged data might result in company misdirection.

The 8mm camera and the supporting media led Kodak to purchase the manufacturer of a major brand of magnetic media, Verbatim, in 1985. Kodak people thought that the media could be coated using the coating technologies of Kodak Park; the magnetic material would be blended in California and then flown to Rochester for coating.

Some say that this was proposed, but was rejected because the change of the magnetic fields of the earth had not been considered. Kodak sold Verbatim in 1992 to Mitsubishi Kasei Corporation, an affiliate of Mitsubishi Corporation. Kodak kept a small format optical disk program and other tape businesses as part of its Mass Memory Division. Kodak was learning about the digital world the hard way even though the people in the acquired companies had the answers but were not asked the needed questions. Was this more Kodak arrogance?

Many if not most of the companies that Kodak acquired during the '80s had little success with integration into Kodak. Many people who headed the companies who came under the Kodak wing said that it was hard to continue their companies in the entrepreneurial style that had made them successful and that had brought them to Kodak's attention.

At Kodak, there was an overwhelmingly great urge to gain efficiency in acquisitions or joint ventures. These efficiencies that might be described by some as the Kodak culture were often the exact ingredients that stifle the benefit of the acquisition in the first place. Each company brought its own unique culture with it to Kodak. Cultures are difficult and even impossible to change sometimes.

Acquired or joint venture companies were required to use Kodak purchasing and human resources (HR). It may have worked well with Kodak but it choked some new entrepreneurial or acquired people. It heavily drained the profitability and efficiency of these infant organizations. The effort to create entrepreneurial companies was soon abandoned by Kodak and almost all those are only notes on the pages of Kodak history.

Kodak executives did not seem to understand small companies. Acquisitions like Eikonix and Atex were mostly closed in 48 months or so. It was a waste of opportunity and a loss of talent that would be felt by Kodak in future years.

Maybe it was the 8AM to 5PM Kodak work ethic that kept Kodak people who visited the newly acquired companies from understanding that the employees of these companies worked at whatever hours were needed to get the job done and that prolonged meetings and discussions, a Kodak style, just took away from productive time.

The great imaging company that made it through 100 years was being challenged from many sides, but initially, it was Japan and Fujifilm that was Kodak's greatest threat. But that was only a beginning challenge; many more companies wanted a piece of the big imaging pie. Kodak's sole line of defense was film.

At the beginning of the 1980s, just as Kodak was approaching its 100th anniversary, a new predator was launched by Japan that was meant to replace film as the way of capturing images. It was not the usual film model but it was an electronic camera that required no film and produced images that could easily be viewed on a home television set.

The Sony Mavica (MAgnetic VIdeo CAmera) was announced on August 24, 1981. To the ordinary observer, it looked like the 35mm cameras of that time. Instead of film, a 2-inch magnetic disk recorded up to 50 analog images. The photos produced were probably best described as single frame television pictures. (Most people have forgotten that TV screen images were made up of two interlaced frames; it made effective use of the TV signal.) Electronic still photography was to be a disruptive new development that Kodak was about to face.

By September of 1982, Sony was showing their new camera, the Mavica, in a closed glass showcase at the Photokina show in Cologne, Germany. To members of the press and selected dealers, Sony, at its German headquarters, was showing not only cameras but also work stations for handling and retouching Mavica images and demonstrating how images could be sent over standard telephone lines from point to point.

Akio Morita, the man who started Sony, was quoted in the press that "Sony would become the Kodak of electronic photography." Morita saw the opportunity of imaging.

Sony did not immediately come out with a product, but Canon marketed their first electronic still camera in mid-1986. While all of these developments were occurring, Kodak kept pointing out that their 35mm film resolution was many times greater than the 280,000 to 380,000 pixel sensors that were in the first electronic still cameras; 35mm film was equal to 15 to 18 million pixels.

The power of film was no benefit to companies like United Airlines that provided the new electronic cameras at all its maintenance locations around the world so that photos of problems could be sent to certified engineers in their San Francisco maintenance facility and these could be used to request instant repair approvals for maintenance and repair advice and formal approval. It kept UA airplanes flying.

Soon, more than a dozen companies were showing electronic still cameras; some even brought them to market. In an effort not to be left behind, Kodak produced some electronic still video components, including a printer and other recording equipment. It was Kodak's acknowledgment of the developing non-silver photography world.

Some suggested that Kodak's best strategy was not to give credibility to the evolving change to their film world. It was not unlike the world that had moved into a new era of technology when the old mainframe computers were replaced with machines that could sit on our desktops and do many of the things that once were film's domain, like typesetting which was now done from an Apple Computer keyboard.

While Apple really began the digital era, IBM's acknowledgment of it gave it a stamp of credibility. Some managers at Kodak saw a similar threat looming for their monopolistic product film, which had brought fat profits for almost a century.

Kodak had been actively pursuing research almost from the time that the first digital imagers were developed in Bell Laboratories. But when you looked carefully at the programs that Kodak spoke about, you discover that only one or two people were involved in specific projects, looking at sensors and other elements, but there was no cohesive effort to take advantage of the developing field of electronic photography.

Some people in senior management began to see Kodak's problem as Filmville Rochester, a small town that did not realize what was happening to the world around it. Rochester had been the place where glass plates were first developed, then films and that was really the only thing that Rochester knew.

Already in the 1980's, suggestions were being made that Kodak should move its headquarters for the new line of electronic products to either Boston or Silicon Valley. Even the mention of this possibility seemed to bring down the wrath of many people on the individuals who dared talk about leaving Rochester.

It was like an act of heresy to think of moving Kodak's headquarters or even part of it out of Rochester. It wasn't many years later that the Consumer Division was moved to Atlanta: with one of the reasons given being Atlanta had better transportation—a major hub airport.

Based on work done in the late 1970's and early 1980's, Kodak was able to fabricate imaging sensors in a small production facility set up in Kodak Research Laboratories. These imagers were originally used in the Kodak Disc-to-film converter device that was shown at 1982 Photokina and later became the basic element that allowed Kodak to create and show its first professional digital camera in 1990 at another Photokina.

A complete line of CCD imaging sensors was developed by Kodak that served machine-vision cameras as well as area array sensors and linear array sensors for scanners and copiers and other applications.

Even before the Clayton Christensen book, *The Innovator's Dilemma: When New Technologies Cause Great Firms to Fail,* appeared, Kodak in the mid-1980s was beginning to recognize that their almost-monopoly businesses, film and paper, were in great peril. Both were highly profitable, up to 75%, something that the electronic business was not.

The list of companies that were acquired by Kodak in the 1980's was like a who's who of the business world covering all the major markets like graphics, magnetic media, optics and business. Names included Atex, Diconix, Eikonix and many more.

In the mid-1980s, Kodak tried to stage what they called, "Blue Sky Fairs." Members of Kodak Research Laboratories were invited to set up tables in the Kodak Office auditorium to show technologies that could lead to future products.

"Blue Sky Fairs" were a great idea but many of the developments were beyond the grasp of Kodak's marketing people while researchers, who had lived mostly sheltered lives in Rochester, knew little of the changing markets that were affecting the company. It was a great idea, but not in Rochester. There was a lot more need at Kodak for broadening experience among both researchers and marketers

It wasn't easy to take Kodak into new directions away from its traditional film base. For example, Kodak, when acquiring Sterling Drugs, was led into an unnecessary competition in purchasing Sterling. Shopping for companies was not Kodak's best suite.

An enterprising Sterling CEO stimulated competition that raised the price that Kodak paid for the company. Many people at the time said that the price should have been $3 billion instead of $5 billion. Much of the enthusiasm for the Sterling acquisition was the potential of using Kodak's very large library of chemical formulas as a resource for discovering new pharmaceuticals.

The problem with much of the Sterling acquisition seems to be the fact that an outside firm did research for

Kodak on pharmaceutical companies that could be considered for the top 10 possibilities for acquisition–Sterling did not make the list. Research suggested that Sterling had no pipeline so future products would be limited.

The valuable part of Sterling was their kitchen product division, but it certainly didn't justify the huge price tag. This resulted in both an overpayment in the purchase price and a limited knowledge of the application of Kodak's chemical library to pharmaceuticals.

It seems that the pharmaceutical industry knew about the formulas in the Kodak library and also knew that many of these formulas already had been discarded because of the potential side effects of the compounds. At times, it appeared that those pushing the move to pharmaceuticals were more concerned about obtaining key positions in possible new organizations than the concern for Kodak and its economic future.

Kodak's electronic business went so far as to establish an electronic division to investigate the possibility of bringing in an outside electronic industry person to head that division, but that was later abandoned when it was realized that Kodak did not yet have enough products to warrant or utilize a person with that expertise.

At the end of 1983, in an effort to take advantage of opportunities that might be outside the charter of its current businesses, Kodak formed a "venture board" to provide venture capital to attract, develop and retain people with entrepreneurial talent within Kodak.

Dr. Bob Tuite was named Director, New Opportunity Development at Kodak. It was an effort to bridge what was developed in research and development and new business opportunities. By the end of 1983, nearly 4,000 ideas had been reviewed and 300 received seed money.

Chairman Colby Chandler in 1985 told employees, "To remain in the vanguard, Eastman Kodak Company will continue to encourage innovation, provide an environment receptive to new ideas and nurture individuals who conceive them, whatever their station in the company. Innovation is not the duty of a select number of employees; rather it is a spirit that should permeate the entire corporation."

More than 100 ideas were commercialized or adopted. Five years later, the survival rate was 9-10% in the idea stage and 30-40% in the business development phase. Fourteen new companies were formed. All were gone in five years.

The most important lessons learned from these ventures was that corporations are far more exposed to damage if the startup company was started outside. Management rewards for an outside startup are usually far greater and so are the risks, of course.

Kodak had sponsored previous Olympics but their $4 million sponsorship of the 1984 Olympics in Los Angeles was outbid by Fuji for the first time. Olympic officials blamed it on the arrogance of Kodak attorneys—one was fired after the games. When it came to television coverage on ABC, Kodak had exclusive rights to TV advertising during the Olympics but because Kodak had spent heavily with ABC for broadcasting, Kodak was the official photographic advertiser for the 1984 Olympics.

Kodak did not have a digital strategy from top-down. Photo CD is a good example. Storage of digital photographs was a problem almost from the inception of digital photography. Digital photographs that were taken in the highest possible resolution assured that large prints could be made in the future, yet they were challenging to transmit and not always in a friendly format.

 Photo CD, developed originally as a consumer storage format, allowed several resolutions of the image to be stored and you could use only the one that best fit your application. This was of great interest to professional photographers.

The product was developed and targeted at the consumer market, a market that was not ready for digitizing images and looking at images on TV. But a commercial and professional market evolved among people like me and some of my professional photography friends.

At that point, what Kodak should have done was mandate, from the beginning, that Photo CD was going to be a portion of their imaging strategy across all the different categories--professional, consumer imaging, printing and publishing. Instead, it became a digital orphan.

Transferring a Photo CD file on a Photo CD was the only way you could make a new one. Its limitations caused the product to disappear. Pricing may also have had a part in the demise of Photo CD. Market plans were based on a Photo CD disk price of $25. The actual market price of blank CDs turned out to be 25 cents or less.

Again, Kodak did not know what it was getting into. A great idea died and took customers down with it who had invested in Photo CD production equipment. It was another loss of credibility for Kodak.

I must have concerned some of Kodak's people by that time because a man was designated to follow me wherever I went in one of their national display booths, because I was "dangerous". It must have been my reports that appeared as a freelancer in the Rochester *Democrat and Chronicle* newspaper.

Kodak asked Sun Microsystems for $1 billion in a law suit involving patents that Kodak acquired from Wang Laboratories in 1977 as part of a $200 million purchase of Wang technologies. Sun settled the patent suit agreeing to license Kodak's patents for $92 million.

Honeywell Inc. filed a patent infringement lawsuit against 34 companies including Eastman Kodak Company related to imaging technology in liquid crystal display screens.

In 1984, the first downsizings occurred in Kodak and were followed almost yearly for years to come. The lifetime job at Kodak was no more. The mindset that developed at Kodak was--outsource everything. Ultimately, even information technology was outsourced to IBM.

Kodak was spending money like heavily in R & D--some in electronics, pharmaceuticals and electronic imaging. Patent suits were becoming a way of life. For most people in marketing, the transition to digital came sooner than they expected. For government business, by 1982, the transition was essentially 100%. Government work was always handled as a separate market area.

For graphic arts, the Apple Computer became sophisticated enough so they replaced the darkroom with digital. Things like typesetting became part of what an Apple computer could do without a darkroom.

Microfilm was another area where the future was limited. Copies of old publications were the main stay of libraries, but even these moved to computer storage with greater and faster searching capability.

In the medical market, for a few years, there were physicians or specialists who insisted on reading everything on film. Soon, MRIs, CAT scans and x-ray films were all digital with copies on CDs or sent to the computer screen of a doctor's office.

Kodak was going to benefit investors only when the business could invest at incremental returns that are enticing; in other words, only when each dollar used to finance the growth creates more than one dollar in long-term market value.

In case of a low return business requiring incremental funds, growth hurts investors. It was evident that Kodak's planned avenues for growth did hurt. Kodak's planned investments were not enticing. Kodak had been at the same place in the '80s when they acquired and dumped a number of firms.

SOME KODAK EQUITY INVESTMENTS

Chinon: cooperative agreement for the manufacture and marketing of 35mm cameras. Kodak also made an equity investment in March 1985. Located in Suwa City, Japan.

ICN Pharmaceuticals: multinational company in the health care field – specializing in pharmaceuticals, research chemicals, and nucleic acid research. In June 1984 Kodak made a minority equity investment in ICN and its subsidiary, Viratek, for the purpose of exploring possible joint opportunities. In April 1985, Kodak and ICN announced a joint research venture, the Nucleic Acid Research Institute, to explore biomedical compounds aimed at stopping the spread of viral infections and slowing the aging process. Based in Costa Mesa, CA.

Viratek: subsidiary of ICN.

Interleaf: In October 1984, Kodak took a minority equity position in Interleaf, a developer of office publishing systems and software products. Supplying the Workstation Publishing System software for the composition end of Kodak Ektaprint Electronic Publishing System (KEEPS). Located in Cambridge, MA.

Sun Microsystems: In October 1984, Kodak took a minority equity position in Sun, a maker of advanced graphics workstations. Furnishing the document composition (graphics) workstations, the text controller, and disk expansion pedestals for KEEPS. Located in Mountain View, CA.

Cauzin Systems, Inc.: agreement announced September 30, 1985 for Kodak to take minority equity position. Kodak was to provide financial backing, along with others, to Cauzin for marketing its Softstrip software system of data storage and transmission. Also, Kodak later announced that it will create Softstrip International with Cauzin for the exclusive rights to market Softstrip media and readers outside North America. Based in Waterbury, CT.

Data Technology Corporation: manufacturer of controllers, the devices which permit a disk drive to interface with a computer. Kodak holds a minority equity position, as part of Atex acquisition, and has an agreement permitting DTC to market the Kodak 3.3 megabyte, 5-1/4" flexible disk drive to systems integrators, OEMs and retailers. Located in Santa Clara, CA.

Elan Corporation: a leader in the specialized health care field of advanced drug delivery technology, concentrating on improved drug absorption. Technology licensing agreement between Elan and Life Sciences Division announced on October 8, 1985. Minority equity position taken by Kodak on October 25. Based in Athlone, Ireland.

Chapter Five–The Kodak Drugstore

When Kay Whitmore became Kodak's CEO, he was a strong advocate of finding a profitable alternative to the photographic film and paper business. He strongly supported the move into the pharmaceutical area, but the Kodak Board was more excited by future potentials of digital products. Whitmore had been chosen as CEO by the Board more because of his gentler people skills. J. Philip Samper, who was passed over as CEO, resigned and went on to be President and CEO of several major California-based digital companies including Sun Microsystems.

Kay Whitmore Kodak CEO 1990-1993

Kodak did a lot of infrastructure investment in China in the 1990s but all the investments were in traditional chemical photography, not digital related. There was a chemical plant, film finishing plant, and traditional camera plants, not a single digital investment. Kodak missed the mark. Samper who had represented the technology track for the company was gone.

Kodak had begun to look at pharmaceutical potentials. The company had made salicylic acid, but anything more than that might have been politically difficult because much of the pharmaceuticals were manufactured in New Jersey and in that state, the U.S. Senate representative protected the pharmaceutical industry.

Kodak Professional Photography Group, using some of the work experience gained from government projects developing digital cameras as early as 1980, showed the first Kodak professional digital camera at the 1990 Photokina.

The camera, based on a Nikon body, was impressive even though the camera was directly connected to a large, heavy, over-the-shoulder box that provided the support and digital storage for the camera; it was a magnificent first effort. That first Kodak professional camera became the turning point for professional photography's move to digital. Later, a model was developed for the Associated Press that changed the world of press photography forever.

1990 Kodak's first pro digital camera

If you had a chance to go behind the scenes to see where this first professional digital camera was built, you would have found that people building it had been given a small space in the vast Kodak Apparatus Division building complex, one of the largest equipment manufacturing plants in Rochester. It was almost as if the effort was to hide the new technology. This certainly wasn't the case, but it would be easy to interpret the small space in that way.

The space also reminded you of where Kodak's much acclaimed first digital camera was built in 1975. Fifteen years later, Kodak built the first professional, portable, color digital camera that would go on to serve the needs of professional photographers around the world.

Since so much work of Kodak's Research Laboratories involved chemistry, there was a continued push to establish presence in the pharmaceutical market. Kodak seemed to be in frenzy, not only with acquisitions establishing divisions to cover some of these future potential areas, but also establishing equity investments, joint enterprises and internal company ventures.

There were some who foresaw the day when Kodak's very high profit photographic film and paper business would have to be matched with profits from other businesses and the pharmaceutical and health areas looked like one of the few places where Kodak could maintain the luxurious profits that it had enjoyed in the past. Going into pharmaceuticals, in the eyes of some people, would be absolutely the worst decision the company ever made but other people at Kodak felt it was the only way to go to maintain the profitability level that had come from film.

In the early 1990s rumors circulated in Rochester that Kay Whitmore, a Mormon, was being considered to replace the late Prophet or leader of the Mormon Church in Salt Lake City. In a conversation with a dealer friend in Salt Lake City, I mentioned the rumor and his comment was, "John, we don't do it that way here in Salt Lake City." Whitmore stayed at Kodak.

The Director of Kodak Research Labs, Jack Thomas, said that Kodak had 80,000 chemicals in the company's inventory and that there had to be four or five of them that might be the best pharmaceuticals in the world. That took the focus off electronics and cost tons of money that pushed up the company debt. If you look at pharmaceuticals in the '80s, they look a lot like photography, very profitable. Growing like a weed, but built on something called the patent race. The first guy gets a patent and the others in the race get nothing.

Kodak had a library of 500,000 untested organic chemicals. Superficially they all looked like they had the right structure to be a potential pharmaceutical, but those who knew something about the business could tell ahead of time that many had lethal side effects. Kodak had developed a useful time release technology but that alone did not make a pharmaceutical business.

By the 1990s, it became apparent that many of Kodak's senior managers did not understand the digital road that was being painted around them. They did not see the linkage between still photographs and motion images that could be seen on home television sets, something that had been demonstrated as early as 1959.

At the end of the '80s, Kodak began to look at core competencies. It was a matter of looking at an industry that was profitable that would use the scope and competencies of Kodak and allow the company to transform away from its consumer photography business. This had been clear in 1980 and even clearer by 1990.

In the January 1992 issue of *New England Business*, a story was told about Kodak's Center for Creative Imaging in Camden, Maine. The article was entitled *Kodak's Peyton Place*. It might make a good-for-TV movie.

The title referred to the movie *Peyton Place* and told a bizarre story about the Kodak people involved in developing and managing the Camden Center. The full story might warrant a complete book, but the highlights were a piece of Kodak's fall from grace.

Kodak's introduction of a Nikon-bodied digital camera in 1990 came with the added burden of both educating and inspiring professional photographers about the use of the camera. Kodak's decades-old Marketing Education Center in Rochester was too mired in politics so an idyllic site was picked by the head of Kodak's Professional Photography Group in Camden, Maine, in 1991. The site, while beautiful, required remodeling and equipping that came to more than $10 million.

The amazing part was that approval was given for the expenditure, including real-estate, in less than a half hour. It was signed by CEO Whitmore and had all the other required signatures. Again, the old boy network worked. Money was easily spent—there were no challenges as to why not use the existing Kodak Marketing Education Center that was by now almost empty. Unneeded millions were spent and would eventually catch up with Kodak.

The Camden (Maine) Center was closed after a couple of years of operation. It was capital hog and equipment technology was changing so fast that Kodak could not afford to re-equip the Center every time there was a perceived need to have the latest and greatest equipment.

CENTER FOR
CREATIVE IMAGING

People from federal agencies who attended the Camden classes liked them so well that many more wanted to attend from the agencies. The head of Kodak's Professional Group did not want the government people in the classes. If government people had been allowed to attend the classes it would have stabilized the Center financially and probably would have taken it profitably well beyond two years of operation.

The Center's director was replaced after a year and the head of the professional group was relegated to close the boondoggle. He was moved to Camden and stayed there until it closed.

It was ironic that at a meeting in Niagara Falls (New York) in the late 1980's to discuss the outlook for the next 50 years for the Eastman Kodak Company, Kay Whitmore, who at the end of the decade would CEO of Kodak, started the meeting with the statement, "Fifty years from now, when your grandchildren hear the name Eastman Kodak, they are going to think of a pharmaceutical company; they are not going to think of an imaging company."

A very few years later, under a new chief executive officer from outside Kodak sold Sterling Drug, to the relief of most Kodak watchers and investors.

To Kodak, analog film and its profits was king, and electronics and digital were either slowed or stopped at every turn. The new electronic and the digital products of the '70s and '80s from other manufacturers, many from outside of the photo industry, were slowly taking away Kodak's recognized leadership as an imaging company.

One example of the company attitude to the changing world came from a Kodak financial analyst who personally detected how the new ways of capturing images were affecting film sales.

When this analyst was in Florida on vacation, he was sitting with his family at an outdoor restaurant as a car full of young people drove by. A person sitting on the back of the convertible was using a camcorder. The analyst suddenly realized that these young people were not using a traditional camera and film, and he wondered if that had anything to do with the noticeable decrease in film sales that he had been observing.

He was lucky. He discovered that Kodak had 150,000 households around the country keeping monthly diary information. It was a little booklet sent out once a month for the participants to keep track of what kind of film they used, where they took their film for processing, and much more. A couple of years before, about 1987, someone had the insight to make an addition to the questionnaire, Have you purchased a camcorder?

When the data was checked, they found that the average person, who had been shooting an average of ten rolls of film prior to buying a camcorder in 1989, now was purchasing only five rolls, after everything had settled down. The analyst counted to himself: ten million camcorders, five rolls of film, which makes fifty million rolls. These were the missing rolls that were no longer showing up on the sales charts.

He was excited and took the information to his boss. He said, "It's not your sales force, it's nothing that you guys are doing, but there is a change in the marketplace and the problem is camcorders. We hadn't been paying any attention to them." He showed the data, but his boss's reply was, "Anybody that knows anything about the film business knows that movie business has never had any impact on still photography." Huh? One more example of Kodak's head-in-the-sand attitude to the changes going on around the company and that would continue to envelop Kodak in the next decade and a half.

The irony to this story is that the boss was released six months later and, because he never signed a non-compete agreement, he went directly to work for one of Kodak's major competitors, Fujifilm. He knew Kodak's weak spots, but he also knew Kodak's customers and he helped Kodak go further out of focus.

The changing world of consumers was one of the greatest challenges for the entire photo industry. You can't stop the consumer from wanting what they want. You have to go with the flow, how can we provide to them the best for them and for the photo industry?

One major photo dealer observed, "Film is just as good as digital and if film had come along now you could call it digital, I think calling the storage medium for digital film today would be a great answer," but the filmcentrics at Kodak shot the idea down..

At the beginning of the 90s Kodak began to talk with Apple Computer about exchanges of technologies. It was the time of the Olympics in Barcelona which Kodak was still sponsoring. It didn't take long to see what the cultures of the two companies were and that Apple's John Sculley and Kodak's Kay Whitmore were both looking down different roads.

Comments that Kodak people had fallen asleep at Apple presentations were not a surprise with past experiences with Kodak's CEO Whitmore. Even though Whitmore was actively promoting the entry of Kodak into the pharmaceutical market, the ever present fear of digital cannibalizing film was there. The talks broke off soon after the time of the Olympics.

Early camera phones gave customers poor quality prints. It wasn't long before the first software (non-Kodak) appeared that significantly improved the prints produced, and of course, the cameras began to rapidly improve so that good prints were possible every time the camera button was pushed. While Kodak was trying to change the "point and shoot" to "point and share," it might have been better if it was "point, shoot, share."

Chapter Six—The Outsider

A member of Kodak's Board said, "We didn't think that Kay Whitmore was the man to head the company for the next 3 to 7 years." Another director said, "This company is very much inbred. That tends to accentuate the faults and also virtues to the point where the virtues become faults. We need a third party to look at Eastman Kodak Company."

Kodak looked outside of the company for a Chief Financial Officer in January 1993. Christopher Steffen, highly regarded by Wall Street, was selected and Kodak stock jumped 36% within two months. Steffen lasted 79 days and Kodak stock dropped 11% the day he left.

Kay Whitmore's role as chief executive office had been a short one. The Kodak Board replaced Whitmore with a new CEO who came from the digital world; he had been CEO of Motorola. George M.C. Fisher was to be the hero who would bring Kodak from its highly profitable film and

George M.C. Fisher Kodak CEO 1993-1999 1

paper world into an uncertain and, at least at the beginning, unprofitable world of digital products.

Fisher had been on the shortlist for consideration as CEO of IBM. Kodak was a much greater challenge because of the company's digital challenges and the need for culture changes that would prove to be the most difficult part of his time in Rochester. George Fisher's wife Ann actively worked to learn all she could about Kodak. Kodak now had a first lady. She visited many locations at Kodak to better understand the company, and she got to know Kodak and Kodak people well.

George Fisher made it clear that his full effort would be to run Kodak. His philosophy was what was good for Kodak was good for Rochester. So he would join only one outside board, only the Board of the Eastman House Museum of Photography, but no universities, schools, or charitable or civic organizations' boards. He would support them, but Kodak got his attention full time.

When George Fisher began his work at Kodak, one of his consultants from outside was John Sculley, Apple's former CEO. Many people wondered about the connection and were further surprised when Fisher hired Carl Gustin to head up the digital functions of Kodak. Gustin had been an assistant to John Sculley.

Gustin lived in Atlanta, Georgia, and made that his headquarters, not Rochester. He never lived in Rochester and commuted there when needed. Ultimately, the consumer marketing headquarters moved to Atlanta as well. They stretched the easy communication lines that had been in place for generations.

Gustin did little to lift the brand value of Kodak which had been deteriorating year-after-year during his watch as Director of Corporate Marketing. Gustin was said to advocate the abandonment of the familiar Kodak yellow box and in one case produced a new film product in a pink and blue box that did not last very long in the market. Unfamiliarity with the look of a new product can produce consumer distrust or suspicions of counterfeited products...

George Fisher saw much promise for growth in the Chinese market, especially for film and printing. Kodak had built manufacturing facilities in China and had sent people from Rochester to help install the equipment and train Chinese personnel. The risk to Kodak was that they may have given up some of their technology to gain access to the Chinese market; it was the Chinese way of doing business.

But China was ready for digital photography and almost completely skipped traditional film, much like they had done with telephones. Cell phones eliminated the need for a wired telephone network. It is a surprise that Fisher who came from the cell phone business had not seen the changes that China had made.

The last Kodak hurrah for analog film was probably the Advanced Photo System (APS) and it occurred on George Fisher's watch. APS was intended to be a new film photo system that was to be partnered with several major Japanese companies. Kodak wanted the Japanese link, first, to find sub-assembly partners for components like flash units; second, to help celebrate the 100th anniversary of the Kodak Brownie film camera, the first real consumer film camera; and finally, to sell the merits of the APS program structure.

The Advanced Photo System program was developed by what was called the "Group of Five": Canon, Fuji, Kodak, Minolta, and Nikon. While analog film and three different image printing sizes were the first part of the original APS concept, there were two additional parts to APS that were never implemented. These included an industry-wide promotion to sell photography and development of an all-digital version of the APS camera. They were great dreams that never happened. Even the letters 'APS' on the new cameras eluded the Group of Five since the letters were trademarked by another company and efforts to acquire clear rights to APS never succeeded.

When George Fisher came to Kodak, he looked around and saw the amount of debt, the fact that Fuji competition was affecting consumer business, and then there was the Disc film camera that had been a fiasco. He could see that film was no longer a great moneymaker. Fisher made up his mind to concentrate on imaging both analog and digital.

Kodak developed a lean production system in 1997 based on Toyota's approach. It was dubbed the Kodak Operating System (K0S). Managers look at everything that happens in terms of waste material, waste of time, and more. They analyzed every step in the process, down to hand movements of assembly-line workers and look for better ways. Everything must create value for the customer. In 1997, it took 100 days for making a film until it reached a customer. With KOS, it took half as long. In 2003, KOS went into the entire Corporation from human resources to product development.

Employees said that micromanaging productivity came on over them like a cloud. Changing the operational parameters drastically is very traumatic. But when an old line company like Kodak tries such an overall change, I am reminded of a trainer we used at Kodak a number of years ago who asked, "How do you eat an elephant?" His answer was, "One bite at a time." Dramatic changes are better done that way—one bite at a time.

The Kodak Image Verification System (Kodak IVS) technology, announced in March 1995, was a process in which a photo of a face could be stored in 400 bits on a credit card. It was a fantastically small use of space–no one had ever done it before. This meant that not only a signature, but also a face of the individual would appear.

IVS was another Kodak product that didn't make it. It was a small example of how things got lost within Kodak.

More than a dozen other announcements made at the same time—all came to an unsuccessful end. Kodak employees were beginning to feel they were expendable. Yet, new financial systems were tightening Kodak business everywhere. But Kodak also needed to remember that new programs needed Kodak people to make them successful.

Getting solid corporate financial information had always been a challenge at Kodak. Finally, Kodak purchased a system called SAP. It covered everything from the purchase and shipment of goods to profit and loss information up to the corporate level. No longer would financial people spend hours gathering information to provide financial data for each level of the company. The ultimate idea being that any manager could access their data and work with the data themselves without intervention or support.

Kodak still had managers who didn't use computers and most of them were the higher level people. When he was CEO, Kay Whitmore did not want a computer in his office. The digital world had not reached him.

The cost of the new system was huge and may have served to create problems with Kodak's customers. When a customer would ask where his product was, or how much it cost, there were no answers to these fundamental questions. It created customer anxieties and probably lost business. At that moment Kodak needed the best of relations with every customer supporting them through the digital transition. It was regrettable that the needs of the Kodak's CFO were ahead of the customer's needs.

Kodak slashed its long-term debt by $6.9 billion from year-end 1993 by selling its Sterling Winthrop pharmaceutical subsidiary, its L and F products household care business, and its clinical diagnostic division which had 1000 employees in Monroe County, New York.

Sterling and some other health related businesses were sold in 1994 and the prescription portion was sold for $1.65 billion, Sterling that had been acquired by Kodak in 1988 for $5.1 billion. Diagnostic imaging was sold for $450 million and the over-counter business was sold for $1 billion.

With the major shift of consumers to cell phone cameras, it became apparent that beginning work with charge-coupled devices (CCDs) hardly a couple of decades after their invention at AT&T Bell Labs, never became more than a small part of Kodak's business. In the meantime, Fuji built a major production facility that could produce sensors for their own cameras that met their design criteria on an ongoing basis.

Kodak continued to announce innovative new image sensors for mass market products such as camera phones and digital still cameras. But Kodak never had a production line for mass production of sensors, only for creating specialty products.

Sony, another major sensor manufacturer, had their own sensor production which came from their original work and producing video cameras. It was evident as Kodak did not link well its research with its manufacturing. It's ironic that the often spoken about invention of the digital camera did not occur in its research laboratories but in a backroom of its manufacturing plant. CEOs of vision were a rarity at Kodak since the days of George Eastman.

OLED (organic light emitting diode), a name for a display technology that Kodak invented but has since sold, was used on one digital camera for viewing photos. The

Kodak EasyShare LS 633 camera was put on sale in Europe, Asia and Australia. With an OLED viewer, the self-luminous pixels did not need a backlight and were viewable in bright outdoor light. Here was an example of technology developed in Kodak Research Labs making it to a product that could open new doors in the world of digital imaging and lighting. Using an OLED panel on another digital camera never happened again. Research and development, marketing and manufacturing were still not on the same page. Each group had separate objectives and needs and coordinating them was a significant concern.

It was sad that George Fisher didn't do more homework before he decided to go legally after Fujifilm in Japan. When he first arrived at Kodak in 1993, he made a personal trip to Japan to see what was going on and he heard what people wanted him to hear not what he should've heard.

Fuji had built very strong alliances with both their dealers and their customers in Japan and Japanese consumers are very loyal. At least one previous Kodak CEO had told their Japan people, "Our mission in Japan is to make trouble for Fuji." It was not the way to build business in Japan.

Kodak distributed all their products through distributors so that Kodak had no real direct contact in the Japanese market or never did any manufacturing in Japan focused on Japanese preferences. Kodak had not done a good job in the Japanese market.

Kodak's attorneys were sure they had a good case and solicited a lot of congressional support, but Kodak's marketing in Japan had not been good. I was very conscious of the Japanese market and its needs since I covered Japan at one point for Kodak. Kodak did well with professional photographers because Fuji products were aimed at the consumer. Japanese customers were loyal to Fujifilm because of the attention paid to them by Fujifilm. Only in more recent years did Fujifilm begin servicing professionals by creating films to meet their specific needs.

Digital photography, when Kodak entered the market, was a fiercely competitive field in which Kodak did not know how to handle the new competitors it was encountering. Kodak had been king in the world of film and color paper for many years, but in digital there were many other names like those at the top of the list like Nikon, Canon, and Sony.

George Fisher had his share of problems but he managed to sell the pharmaceutical business that had been acquired, the copier business, and shed the Eastman Chemical Company. However, there were important lessons to be learned in shedding assets.

Many companies have rushed to break up and spin off divisions that possibly management didn't understand or they faced the pressure of stockholders to unlock hidden assets. Sometimes it is better to hold onto an asset like Eastman Chemical Company and possibly the health businesses that could be sold later but Kodak needed to provide the structure that might have allowed the company to continue in business and prosper. There are risks in every decision we make, some very clear and others that will become apparent later. It is that depth of vision and strength of purpose that makes a noteworthy CEO.

When Kodak looked at digital trends, you had to wonder if they ever read recent trade publications. Statistical modeling is almost useless if not checked against current collected data that is commonly published even in trade publications. Over the years, Kodak internal data, too often, was what managers wanted to hear rather than reality of what was happening. That may explain some of Kodak's reluctance to move from traditional film to digital in a variety of fields like consumer, professional, industrial, medical and commercial printing.

It was a $50.5 million acquisition in cash for OREX Computed Radiography Ltd. OREX manufactured and marketed compact CR systems for specialty markets such as orthopedics, diagnostic imaging centers and dentistry. It opened another market for Kodak, servicing industrial non-destructive testing (NDT). Kodak had been building a very respectable health business, but it would not be long before all of it would be sold.

Kodak had not forgotten professional digital photography. Its sensor group produced new sensors with 39 million pixels and another with 31.6 million pixels designed for professional cameras. Kodak has spent more than 100 years helping people preserve their memories. Now it was up to Kodak to preserve its own legacies if it could.

Much attention had been given over the last 30 years to diversity at Kodak. In May of 1999, Kodak responded to the internal complaints about racial and gender discrimination and paid out $13 million to female and minority employees in New York and Colorado. It was another area that Kodak had not kept in focus. The happy world of Kodak was being shaken by the culture that was evolving around it.

When Fisher came to Kodak, he signed a five-year contract and then agreed to a two-year extension which got him to age 60. He promised his wife that he would do something else at 60. He said "If I really thought that I could have finished the job, whatever that means, in two or three years, I probably would've stayed, but I didn't. I thought this is not a forever journey, but it was going to be a 5 to 10-year journey to get Kodak into position in the digital world."

"Well, as in every industry, your strengths become your weaknesses as you transition and the strength of Kodak was being the world leader in film production and marketing and in paper. That was a franchise that was the envy of the world and just as in Clayton Christiansen's work on disruptive technology; you have the culture of a company trying to protect the thing that makes all the money even as other alternatives come in." (From my last George Fisher interview after his retirement.)

George Fisher also did not miss the challenges that Kodak's culture had developed over more than 100 years. It was especially challenging to the first CEO in many years to join the company from outside. He felt it was something he could not change in his lifetime.

Fisher was right. Cultures in companies like Kodak are better served working with them rather than changing them. Many times, company cultures are used to cover worker attitudes or deficiencies, Fisher, and yes, even his wife Ann, the wonderful diplomat, tried hard to effect changes, but they had limited results.

Chapter Seven—Another Kodak Man From Inside

Dan Carp is a man who was always available to the people he knew. More of Carp's time with the Eastman Kodak Company was spent in international markets, including Canada, Europe and Latin America than any other part of his work.

People knew that Carp was marked for special things when he was selected as Kodak's Sloan Fellow, a role that has marked each person attending Sloan from Kodak as a potential leader of Kodak. The singular use of one school may have limited the view of people who were to be the potential future leaders within Kodak. The hiring of George Fisher as Kodak's CEO was a move by Kodak's board to change that model, but not a completely successful one. But now, Kodak was back to the insider track for CEO's.

Carp was approachable, but he differed from his predecessor, George Fisher. My personal remembrance was that if I saw a new product or trend and dropped a note to George, Fisher replied to every note and memo that reached him with a few words in longhand. Carp did not seem interested in that quick approach. Yet, he was very approachable and listened well to what was happening on his watch.

Dan Carp Kodak CEO 2000-2005

Carp was more like the typical Kodak-bred individual who keeps their playing cards close, except at local poker get-togethers—there were a lot of those in Rochester. Carp moves easily in top executive circles, yet is readily available to employees or friends. It was my pleasure to be considered a friend of Dan Carp because he was always willing to listen.

It was Dan Carp's first year as CEO, at a conference in Boston, he was betting the company on digital. His predecessor, George Fisher, came with technology credentials as Kodak's CEO but he never came close to having digital as the major part of Kodak's business and profitability. What Carp had going for him were film profits which were still there through much of his time as CEO.

It was amazing to see that at the beginning of the 2000s, many people were still envisioning the handheld digital camera as being the way people would capture pictures. Growth in cell phone cameras was significant but there was still a need for higher resolution and easier ways of either storing or transmitting pictures, those were yet to come.

In the Kodak 2000 annual report, Dan Carp's first as CEO, (they didn't even date the cover–perhaps that was a sign of Carp times?) Kodak had begun a campaign to identify their business as 'infoimaging'. Some people at Kodak were trying to create a new and better description for Kodak's broad business line.

When I asked financial analysts if this was to better clarify Kodak's potential, most laughed and said that it didn't do anything for Kodak. On a flight into Rochester one day, I asked the passenger next to me, the CEO of a building supply company, if he knew what 'infoimaging' meant? He said that he didn't know, so I explained the term to him. His simple reply was, "I don't 'infoimage', I take pictures."

It was a lesson Kodak forgot. While the imaging portion was correct, there were many more specific aspects to imaging. 'Info' really did not fit nor did people understand the word.

A simple admonishment, KISS or "Keep it simple, stupid," could have helped.

Carp inherited his own albatross, not unlike the Ancient Mariner. When the Kodak Marketing Education Center (MEC) in Rochester, New York, was opened in 1971, one of the speakers told a story about his three brothers and a sister. One night the father announced that the sister was going to the Olympics in Germany and they would all have to work hard to support her trip. There was some grumbling; the boys said they couldn't afford it, but the father's reply was that each family can afford one princess.

And that is what the speaker called Kodak's new MEC. From that day on, it was always referred to as the princess or jewel of Kodak. The jewel had its detractors because of the architect's choice of steel that rusts and was supposed to develop a lasting patina.

However, the patina never happened at the MEC building because in its country location there were few pollutants to help stop the rusting. MEC never wound up with a beautiful color finish—maybe it was a sign of things to come.

Apparently the original MEC designs that called for thermal windows were replaced with single pane glass and in the cold Rochester winters and hot summer days, temperatures were difficult to control, it was cold in the winter and in the summertime it was very warm near the windows. MEC was very expensive to maintain.

It was designed of rusty steel to be built in Arizona and the big overhangs around the building were to keep the sun from coming in; it just rusted. It took a lot of money just turning over the rocks that were underneath it so that the rusting didn't show as it ran off the building every time it rained.

Yet, it was a spectacular building that Kodak used well at the time. It was politics that brought most training to a stop with the exception of one of Kodak's favorite topics: diversity training.

The buildings were put up for sale and Kodak finally told Rochester Institute of Technology, President Dr. Al Simone that Kodak was planning to make a gift of MEC to the school. RIT could find some great uses for the facility and already owned the adjacent property to MEC.

But that was never to be. One day, a visitor from Kodak visited Dr. Simone and told him that Kodak was not going to give the buildings to RIT and instead presented the school with a gift check for $2 million. No other explanations were given. RIT was happy with the gift.

A local business group tried to buy MEC in the mid-90s and lease it back to Kodak. They were told that Kodak would never sell its crown jewel of education and training. Today it sits rusting as another example of poor Kodak planning.

Kodak finally sold the property for $3.5 million. That included more than 300,000 square feet of buildings plus 150 acres surrounding the buildings with a tax evaluation of $11.2 million. Today the buildings sit empty. The "Princess" is another reminder of Kodak's past greatness sitting empty and deserted, not unlike its parent Kodak.

The challenges of what people would do with their digital photographs dogged Kodak for a number of years. Photo shops with their digital minilabs were successors to the film versions but with added capabilities of not only producing prints but CDs, and a wide variety of merchandise in some cases like coffee cups and medallions just to mention a few.

Not everyone had the capability of doing prints at home or the patience required to both upload digital photos and create a final product with what the home person thought was acceptable quality. Kodak had color photo papers for laboratory processing but also thermal color papers that could be used in both minilabs and home printers.

Kodak entered the new millennium with plans to cut 20% of its payroll. Competitor Fuji continued on and both Kodak and Fuji were facing heavyweight digital competitors like Sony, Nikon, Canon, Panasonic, Samsung and others.

Kodak was a stock for the most patient of investors and even they would run out of patience.

Carp's first Kodak President, Patricia Russo, left after only nine months on the job to head up Lucent and he replaced her in April 2003 with Antonio Perez who turned HP's Printing Division into a $10 billion dynamo. When Perez arrived he said that Kodak had digital technology coming out of its ears. What was missing was focus. He identified three areas of concentration: consumer imaging, health imaging and commercial printing.

In 2003, Kodak still had a decent position in the medical, entertainment, and government imaging markets and where the margins were still reasonable. The film business was still growing outside of the US. Statements like, "we have a balanced strategy for growth" and "we will finance the strategy for growth" were Kodak management's response to questions about the future.

By 2003, 70% of Kodak's operational leadership group came from outside of Kodak. Just three of the 11 executives on the leadership chart rose through the ranks at Kodak, the three were long insulated from outside influences. But several of the outside leaders had come with Antonio Perez from HP giving them limited depth, not unlike Kodak-trained leader's digital experience in many cases.

In September of 2003, Eastman Kodak Company slashed its generous $1.80 annual dividend to $.50 a share, the first cut in a century.

For the health markets, Kodak developed the Kodak secure E-Mail Services to expedite secure communications between approved parties and it replaced expensive and time-consuming package delivery services for medical records, x-ray images and related patient information. Kodak was still building its health group.

The first system was purchased by a local Rochester organization, the Unity Health System, a 681-bed healthcare network. More work was needed on the Kodak product since competitors offered more healthcare codes and better performance. It appeared that Kodak had not done enough homework on the product.

Kodak stopped promoting, "You've got pictures," its project with America Online.

It was a repositioning of product lines for Kodak's Commercial Imaging Group (CIG) when its largest unit, Remote Sensing Systems, was sold by Perez to ITT Industries, Inc. for $725 million. Perez pulled Kodak out of other partnerships as well. Perez was reshaping Kodak to his liking.

In Time magazine, Kodak CEO Dan Carp was quoted as saying, "I'm one of those people that has to have change." Kodak's film business was in free-fall. Kodak had been talking digital for many years but not delivering. The change was there for Carp to grasp.

Kodak completed the acquisition of Algotec Systems Ltd. at the end of 2003. Algotec, a developer of medical imaging equipment, had 70 employees worldwide and was based in Israel.

Kodak agreed to buy Scitex Digital Printing, a subsidiary of Tel Aviv for $250 million in cash. Scitex digital printing, Dayton, Ohio is expected to add $190 million in revenue in its first year as a Kodak subsidiary. This is another step on the path for Kodak to commercialize its proprietary inkjet technology.

At the end of 2003, Kodak announced a new leadership team and operating model. Kodak was trying to make business sense from the company's legal and sales efforts. It was quite a shuffle, Kodak trying to find the right mix of people.

To increase Kodak's control of its commercial printing business, Kodak purchased Heidelberg's 50% interest in NexPress Solutions, a 50/50 joint venture of Kodak and Heidelberg. At closing, Kodak would pay over a two-year period up to a maximum of $150 million in cash. Kodak had gone back to try again.

At the 2004 Consumer Electronics Show, a panel of experts was still saying that digital cameras would be the primary method of picture capturing images near term.

That message was quickly changed by the Apple iPhone and it's easy to use software to handle the images.

By 2004, Dan Carp, Kodak's CEO appearing on national television, did not express confidence. Staff cuts would eliminate 12,000-15,000 more jobs.

In the fourth quarter 2004, Kodak took the top spot in US market share for digital cameras. It was the first time that Sony had been passed.

You have to wonder about the confused information supplied to Dan Carp. Speaking at a national meeting in 2005, Carp expressed concerns for camera phones not producing enough quality. Apparently, he was not aware that eight megapixel cameras would soon be in many or most phones and future pad devices. It was a sign of the limited vision and thinking that was guiding Kodak.

Kodak was looking for industry partnerships with the first announced as a 10-year cross-licensing and marketing arrangement to supply Motorola with Kodak CMOS sensors. It wasn't long before Kodak sold off their sensor business.

Even the use of digital photographs in court rooms became a challenge. Once upon a time, when a photograph made with film was introduced, it was simply the word of the photographer in court that gave credibility to the acceptance of the photograph. People are well aware today that a digital photograph can be easily manipulated with Adobe Photoshop or other software with a significant chance that the evidence submitted would be challenged with likelihood that it might not be accepted by a judge.

Technology brings a lot of new terms. Terms sometimes impress the people who invest in these companies. Megapixels was the first digital term many people learned when it came to digital cameras. Kodak's historic first digital camera from 1975 had 10,000 pixels; it was a long way from the megapixel sensor that showed up in the first Kodak professional camera, the DCS.

Twelve to sixteen megapixel cameras are common and there have been a few people who put together multi-megapixels for scientific applications. The megapixel issue has gone to bed but there's a lot more that can be done with electronic digital imaging.

At the Kodak 2004 annual meeting, Dan Carp was still saying that there was a dynamic and positive future for the company. Antonio Perez identified 50,000 Kodak kiosks as being in place worldwide and health had grown. He also indicated that Kodak was abandoning the Advanced Photo System which was developed in the late 90s. Perez also announced the sale of the remote sensor area of the business. It was going to ITT. Kodak was still slimming down.

In the early 2000's, Kodak began to sense that their role as leading provider of film stock was facing an uncertain future because of digital. Kodak purchased LaserPacific Media for $30.5 million as a wholly-owned subsidiary to provide postproduction services for Hollywood. Kodak already had Cinesite which also provided services for the motion picture industry. If film disappeared, Kodak could still offer services to Hollywood. Kodak sold LaserPacific Media in 2010.

Perez's service at HP was primarily in printing and he left soon after Carly Fiorina became HP CEO. Perez wanted to head printer programs for HP. Carly saw some shortcomings in Perez like a lack of tact and his inability to read people. Certainly Perez did not understand the culture of the company he was about to join, the Eastman Kodak Company.

Kodak realigned all of the leadership roles in 2003. Dan Carp no longer had any connection to any operating unit. All units reported to Antonio Perez. There would be a business area called commercial printing which brought a new perspective to digitally driven commercial printing. Kodak would no longer be a film business.

Kodak acquired PracticeWorks Inc., a leading provider of dental practice management software (DPMS) and digital radiographic imaging systems in July 2003. Kodak will also become 100% owner of Paris-based subsidiary Trophy Radiologic, a developer of dental digital radiography equipment that PracticeWorks acquired the previous December. Kodak was building a portfolio of companies for the health market that would meet future digital needs.

The 2004 PMA show in Las Vegas, Nevada, was to be the last one for CEO Dan Carp. He said, "As a manufacturer, we can at least partly see the future by watching the technological flow. Unlike photo retailers, photo finishers, and professional photographers, we know what our R & D Department is working on, we can see what patents are being filed, and gain an idea of where the market is going. Our customers can't do that, but they need to invest. That's why they need an advisor they can trust. We at Eastman Kodak are working hard to be that advisor."

At the same PMA show, Kodak COO Antonio Perez indicated that his entire professional career was in digital. When he came to Kodak he found that things exceeded his most optimistic expectations. There was a wealth of very powerful digital and intellectual property. He was expecting to commercialize the technology he found very quickly. Certainly Kodak's wealth of patents did not result in enough developments to sustain Kodak.

Continued restructuring brought challenges to Kodak and to its customers. Kodak people that knew and worked well with customers were moved or gone. People without customer experience did not understand how important it was to maintain their contacts with customers.

A new combined Customer Imaging and Professional Imaging Organization marketed products such as consumer cameras, one-time use cameras, consumer and professional films were to be part of the capture business while products such as kiosks, professional lab solutions and professional thermal printers, retailed minilabs solutions, photographic paper, and wholesale operations would be grouped in output businesses. Only time would tell if the effective use of people would result in satisfied customers.

Kodak made a number of moves to make their healthcare information systems a world leader. World headquarters for the Health Care Information Systems (HCIS) was located in Rochester as one of six strategic product groups within health imaging; Kodak was looking at all the systems, software, hospital radiology departments and imaging centers.

Certainly it was easy to see that this could be expanded to entire hospitals or multiple locations within the community. R&D spending included several acquisitions as well as a relocation of assets and spending to produce the best possible results. Kodak was making the investments because the healthcare marketplace represented a significant global opportunity for Kodak. Here was another one of the major opportunities for Kodak, but later it was sold.

Kodak's Health Imaging Group products found their way even to the remote regions of the Brazilian rain forest. A medical group used digital manager medical imaging technology in the form of Computer Radiography (CR) and a picture archiving and communication system to acquire digital medical x-ray images of tribe members and send these via satellite to a state-of-the-art radiology clinic in southern Brazil where digital, no-chemistry processes would be used in an area of the world that needed preserving.

Even as Kodak saw the falloff in consumer film imaging, Kodak produced *Definition of the Great Picture,* a guide featuring Sarah Ferguson, the Duchess of York. The filmcentric views of Kodak still ruled over digital. Had Kodak management understood digital better, perhaps this would've been a film/digital book fitting the transitional time it was published.

The stability of digitally printed prints on a variety of papers and possibly using a variety of inks has the potential of raising issues like dye fading that occurred some 50 years ago to traditional silver halide color paper. Today, there is more than one choice for inks, some developed by manufacturer of the printer, but in papers there may be many choices, and each will produce a different final color print. There may be even more variability in the fading of those digital color prints.

Printing at home has been too much of a challenge for some people so they use outside sources for printing. These outside sources could have a number of variables that could ultimately result in prints fading or changing colors because of either where they were placed or the environment in which they were placed. This will be future challenges for manufacturers and suppliers.

Sometimes you have to wonder about the licenses that a large manufacturer must take for a product that might never happen. Kent Displays Incorporated licensed its cholesteric "No Power" LCD technology to Kodak. The technology enabled changeable displays that maintained images indefinitely without consuming power and can be viewed at a wide angle and a range of lighting conditions. A neat idea but it was another sign that Kodak did not have its digital thinking together.

It's sometimes interesting to go back and look at things that you have written and forgotten about. A decade ago in one of the local Rochester newspapers I wrote a guest essay that said: "Will anyone understand Kodak's 'info-imaging'? Or will that be another Photo CD? That was a Kodak digital product of a decade ago for storing photos that resorted to infomercials on television to come to explain what its benefits were and how it worked. But that product never made it into the consumer's homes. Time will tell, and there is not too much of that in today's world for companies like Kodak."

In a press interview in 2004, that companies were taking good money out of corporations and investing in accounting requirements, Kodak had done just that with the advent of the SAP system which produced information that was reliable worldwide and quickly; however, customer service and customer records fared very badly and probably accounted for some of Kodak's lost business.

Kodak was late in adopting computers the way others have. For example, Fuji had developed computerized control in the manufacturing of products in the '70s and '80s while Kodak was still using 3 x 5 cards and sorting those for manufacturing blends of color paper and other information.

In a guest essay, CEO Carp said, "Kodak has a new, more competitive cost structure that will keep us far less vulnerable to predatory price wars. And, Kodak has the brand name that means pictures to everybody, a brand name that every technology company, every old and new economy company would love to partner with." Apparently Carp did not know how Kodak's brand value had fallen over the years to a point where by the end of the decade, Kodak's brand value would not even be in the top 100 brand lists any longer.

Speaking at Kodak's annual get-together for institutional investors for the first time as Kodak's CEO, Dan Carp indicated that 45% of its annual revenue would come from digital by the end of the year; this was based on signed contracts from dot-coms. Little did he know that Silicon Valley would be picking up debris from the failure of many dot-coms. The old adage still applies, "A little learning is a dangerous thing." That is especially true in the digital world.

Every Kodak quarterly report in the last dozen years has been a moment of agony. In the third quarter of 2000, CFO Bob Brust was quoted as saying, "We had a big derailment here and were frightened trying to find out what it was." This was just after a new financial data system was installed at Kodak worldwide so that good information was available on a real-time basis.

Unfortunately, so often these multimillion dollar systems did not take into account some of the practical considerations that people have experienced. Kodak had low debt, good margins and was stable and healthy. Certainly digital was infringing on Kodak's long time cash cow film, but the company was making good progress.

Kodak missed the boat when low end of digital cameras were first introduced. By then, Kodak had an R & D lab in Japan that offered to help with the first camera designs. They were told that, "The cameras must be black and look different." The filmcentrics were again at work.

Kodak had some beautiful camera designs but the prices were above where the market was moving. Kodak finally produced its first consumer camera, the Kodak Digital Science DC 40. Finished in black and priced at $600, it was well over what the average consumer would pay. No sense competing with an inexpensive film camera.

When Dan Carp became CEO he wanted to make Kodak into a digital imaging enterprise with three parts: consumer photography, commercial printing, and medical technology. Kodak's market value had dropped severely and plans were made to eliminate 21,000 jobs. As one financial analyst described it, Carp had become a juggler and was trying to keep all the balls in the air, not an easy feat in the market at that time, or any time.

Kiosks are one product that exceeded Kodak's profit model with an average margin of 30%; the actual margins ran as high as 150% to 200%. Over the years, strong competition developed for this marketplace with several major manufacturers including Sony providing competitive kiosks and thermal dye transfer material for printing. One specialty kiosk was developed and printed only photo books for customers.

Kodak introduced the Kodak Cinema Server to decrypt, decompress and send feature-length content to any projector up to 2K resolution. Kodak was also selling their Kodak Digital Cinema advertising systems that operate as preshow information and advertising packages. Kodak had many opportunities to make up for motion picture print stock that would disappear in the next few years.

There was an expansion in Kodak's commercial printing business: from Heidelberg in Germany, Kodak purchased the remainder of Kodak NexPress Solutions LLC, their joint venture with Kodak and also Heidelberg's NexPress GmbH, Heidelberg's German subsidiary. The cost to Kodak: a maximum of $150 million in cash. The acquisitions would be a combined operation in Rochester.

Working with IBM, Kodak recognized the opportunity that healthcare information technology was worth $60 billion a year and growing. The two firms worked to develop computer systems to manage radiology and related records in smaller hospitals and imaging centers.

When you hear comments from the General Manager for Kodak's Digital Cinema that "Nothing captures color and the nuance of imagination better than film; there is no other medium that, in the hands of a talented cinematographer, offers a greater range of story-telling possibilities," it certainly sounded like the 1980 defense of color film photography when digital photography was born. Kodak had not learned the changing lessons of the times. Cinematography classes in California universities have been teaching the use of digital cinema photography for a decade. The new crops of cinematographers are well-prepared for the exit of traditional film.

Kodak had been part of the Dow Jones stock market index since 1930. In 2004 Kodak was replaced on the Dow by companies that better represented the market. Kodak had been passed over. It was a sign of Kodak's loss of value and recognition.

Dan Carp retired in 2005 and in his final prepared statement he said, "I wouldn't leave if we had not laid the foundation for the transition." Many observers thought that it is why Perez came to Kodak after missing the CEO role at HP.

For Kodak, its often cited arrogant style of management may have had other implications that have shown up in recent times. It was a very small amount, but a number of people are facing criminal charges for a scheme that lasted 13 years and cost Kodak $14 million. Two executives in Kodak's Tax Department were involved with 160 unauthorized contracts. There was no documentation, invoices, purchase orders or the like for numerous payments. It was another warning message for Kodak, "Who's minding the store?"

Kodak, at one time, conducted classes in business ethics for its employees to be sure that everyone understood clearly that large corporations were then and would always be under outside observation for its business conduct.

Chapter Eight—The Printer Man

Antonio Perez's came to Kodak with his own mantra:

---

1. See the future through the eyes of your customer.

2. Intellectual property and brand power-- our key assets

3. Use digital technology to create tools for customers

4. Build a championship team not a group of champions

5. Innovation is a state of mind

6. Speed is critical, so push your organization

7. Partner up if you're not the best in something

After Carly Fiorina became CEO of HP, Antonio Perez had wanted to become head of all printers. Instead Carly appointed another woman in charge and that gave him his reason for leaving HP. He went to another company and ultimately to Kodak.

If Kodak knew more about Antonio Perez, they might have taken little more time making a decision. Perez was said to not read people well, he did not understand that companies had different cultures, and most things he did were at the superficial level. At a large HP company dinner at a country club, Perez was invited to speak and he proceeded to try to be humorous with a joke that was not fit for mixed company. This was the individual that Kodak's Board brought in first as President and then as CEO of the company and finally to Bankruptcy Court.

What will probably be remembered most about Antonio Perez, in his role as CEO of Kodak, will be the 75 minutes he spent on the telephone with Kodak directors deliberating on making Kodak's bankruptcy Chapter 11 filing. After the 75 minute discussion, at 4:48 PM Wednesday, January 18, 2012, the Eastman Kodak Board of Directors voted to file for Chapter 11 bankruptcy. The documents were filed shortly after midnight and people in Rochester awoke to find Chapter 11 headlines in their morning newspaper. Certainly the remaining 5,000 Rochester employees were shaken.

Frank Romano, Rochester Institute of Technology Professor Emeritus, commented that, when it comes to technology, "I would like them to stop adding features. There's a new version coming out this summer. It's amazing," he says. "The world was changing faster than old-line companies like Kodak could handle."

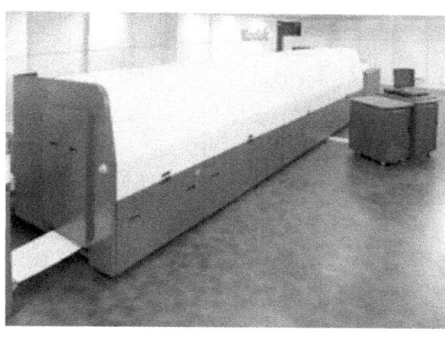
Kodak Prosper XL Press

Romano provided a little bit of output history. He went through the list of technologies, including toner, inkjet, solid ink, and so on. "Inkjet has grown up like crazy. It used to fade away right there." He added, "Kodak just bought a company to get them back to where they were in 1989!" It was one of the several printing equipment companies Kodak repurchased that Romano referred to.

Looking back, Romano said that 30 years ago he saw inkjet as the future of the printing industry, but he cannot understand why it has taken so long to develop, particularly in an age of instant gratification. "We live in an on-demand society. Now we complain if we have to wait one hour (for prints)." Everything has to be fast, from quick printers to the 1-hour photo labs, self-ticketing, and do-it-yourself kiosks.

Kodak thought they had a winner in 2003 when they bought the assets of Applied Science Fiction (ASF) that had developed a non-chemical way of getting images from film and putting them onto a CD. The only catch was that the film was destroyed in the process. Kodak spent an estimated $50 million for the acquisition, and soon dumped the entire project and took a charge of $45 million in closing ASF a year later. What Kodak people did not realize was that there was much other software that had been developed by ASF that had the potential for licensing and even further development.

Antonio Perez Kodak CEO 2005-Present

Kodak spent $817 million to buy Sun Chemicals 50% share of Kodak Polychrome Graphics which sold film-based digital products to the graphic printing industry. Kodak had sold that 50% to Sun in the '80s and now, as Romano had said earlier, Kodak was back to where they were in 1989.

Antonio Perez came to Kodak as the architect of a new digital Kodak. It was amazing that in his first visit to Kodak research labs he had some surprises in inkjet printing technology even though he had come from Hewlett-Packard that was known for that capability. I remember when I was on a personal press tour of KRL that a number of researchers told me of the visit by Perez and the satisfaction he got from how much digital progress Kodak researchers had already made.

One of the challenging sides of digital photography is today's ever presence of cell phone cameras of good quality as well as pocketable cameras of even superior quality. The Abu Ghraib prison pictures from Iraq showed the world the bad side of what has been accomplished in the country. But that is the immediacy of digital photography and the Internet.

One of the challenging sides of digital photography is today's ever presence of cell phone cameras of good quality as well as pocketable cameras of even superior quality. The Abu Ghraib prison pictures from Iraq showed the world the bad side of what has been accomplished in the country. But that is the immediacy of digital photography and the Internet.

Some Kodak Plant Closings

Kodak's single use camera plant in Rochester, NY, closed in July 2003 laying off 500 people. Production was moved to China.

Sensitizing operations were closed in April 2003 in Guadalajara, Mexico, costing 500 jobs.

150 jobs were lost when Kodak closed its Citipix business in Quebec City.

In 2004, Kodak contracted to demolish 24 buildings totaling 1.3 million ft.^{2} of space in the Rochester Kodak Park complex. Savings would include tax savings from reduced assessments, lower heating and cooling costs, reduced insurance costs and lower maintenance and capital spending. Kodak had already torn down 56 older buildings and structures.

Kodak in June 2004 broke ground for a $40 million thermal media and inkjet plant in Colorado. The target for opening was spring of 2005.

Kodak Australia closed its Coburg film and photographic paper plant in November 2004 which put 600 production workers out of work. The Kodak Australia Wholesale Lab closed October 22, 2004 with 300 more administrative jobs lost in March 2005.

Printing plate manufacturing operation in Colorado and converting and packaging facilities for motion picture films were shut down in early 2009 affecting 300 employees. The Columbus, Georgia, plant will pick up plate production and Rochester will pick up motion picture film work. Colorado would continue to make thermal media for digital print kiosks and color photographic paper use for photofinishing. After the closures, Windsor, Colorado will have 400 fewer workers, down from 1600 prior to the sale of an x-ray film processing unit there in 2007.

Manufacturing sites in England and France were affected in March of 2005 by Kodak's changing image. Harrow, England was to remain a major site for the production of color photographic paper and sensitizing graphic arts film. This affected 250 jobs.

The Annesley (England) plant that made consumer photographic products closed in 2005 affecting 350 jobs.

Chalon (France) continued to make health imaging and motion picture print film products but consumer films and color photographic paper ended in September of 2005 with the loss of about 270 jobs. It was a tough business.

Kodak announced in 2005 that its paper mill that had been producing high-quality papers for photo applications for 40 years was to be closed in 2005. Plant managers were given six months to sell the machinery. No buyers were found in that short time so holes were drilled in the high precision rollers of the machines and they were all scrapped.

Kodak built a thermal dye paper manufacturing line and installed it in the former paper mill building. In April 2012, the thermal

dye plant was closed in Rochester and production moved to
Colorado.

It cost Kodak $27 million in severance costs, exit costs and
accelerated depreciation to close five overnight photofinishing
labs in France.

*To the men and women who worked on these machines
or environs, it was a painful experience. Those ordering
the closings had little concern for the pride and dedication
of Kodak workers throughout the world.*

Kodak's Health Imaging Group served the global
healthcare community for more than 100 years. Kodak had
innovative computed radiography (CR) systems and long
length imaging systems that enhance the quality of patient
films, shorten the time interval for delivery, reduced
retakes, and it enabled the radiologist to digitally view
patient medical images. It was a natural for the growth of
Kodak's many years as a reliable medical community
supplier of x-ray films, processors, and chemicals.

The potential for medical imaging and systems was
already evident in 2004 with orders for five Buffalo, New
York, hospitals, for Kodak's innovative computed
radiography (CR) systems and Long-Link imaging systems.
Kaleida Health had tried several systems prior to making
the selection of Kodak. Image quality and the Kodak
service team made the difference.

The healthcare business that Kodak had built over the
years which had $2.7 billion in revenues in 2005 was now
going on the sales floor. While denying that selling the
business was to meet borrowing needs, named one of three
pillars of Kodak in 2003, Perez indicated it was the least
promising of the three, consumer photography and printing
industry supplies being the other. Perez's feelings were that
Kodak was rooted in 19th Century business models which

made it hard for him to do anything. Possibly some of that may also have been due to Perez's limited background. As one industry analyst described it, "now Kodak had a two legged stool."

Perez would soon bring to Kodak more of his HP friends in key roles like Jim Langley as President of Commercial Printing, another old associate from HP.

It didn't take long for Antonio Perez to build his new executive team. In the fall of 2003, just three of 11 top executives shown on the organization chart shared with investors had come up through the ranks at Kodak.

When he became CEO, Perez brought HP inkjet veteran, Bill Lloyd, as his Chief Technical Officer and Director, Research and Development. He had been Co-Chief Executive Officer of Phogenix Imaging, a joint effort between HP and Kodak. That effort had resulted in an inkjet minilab that appeared in the spring of 2002. Phogenix was dissolved a few months later.

Kodak, at the 2004 Photokina in Cologne, Germany, had a huge display hall and nothing but some photos of pretty ladies and a few small tables of products. In an article that appeared in *Photo Industry Reporter*, I described the Kodak booth as the best display of Pergo flooring that I had seen. Later I found out that Kodak did not hesitate to tell a financial analyst friend that Kodak had saved $14 million by not only cutting the display but also the staff that represented Kodak.

Fujifilm at the same show had a large well-equipped booth with a variety of new equipment, digital and film cameras, film and many other products. It was no coincidence that adjacent to the Fuji booth was the Fuji Xerox booth with a variety of digital printing equipment that would be needed by growing large laboratories. Fuji representatives, on their own time, went to educational sessions so they could help dealers who couldn't attend the sessions.

Some believe that the statement that Antonio Perez made in 2006 that Kodak was "not headed for a breakup" was interpreted by many Kodak watchers as meaning that Kodak was already well on the path to breaking up the company.

It was evident that Perez was trying to break away from the traditional photo business. It had been a tradition that when a new president had been elected to the presidency of the Photo Marketing Association International (PMAI), the president and the executive secretary of the group would visit Rochester to meet with Kodak's CEO. After Perez became CEO the PMAI was informed that Perez only had time for financial analysts or writers, not for PMAI people.

Antonio Perez, at the 2006 Consumer Electronic Show, described digital cameras as dinosaurs, not evolving as fast as the ecosystems around them. Rather than embrace new technology the industry has been encumbered by its analog past, simply swapping "silicon for silver". It was a hard indictment of an industry that had been led astray by the very company Perez worked for, Kodak.

Kodak had never prepared itself for any manufacturing of sensors or other related digital products that would make Kodak competitive in the style that once had been Kodak's hallmark− manufacturing complete units from start to finish in Rochester. Kodak had used IBM to create imagers, and then Taiwan Semi-Conductor Manufacturing Company Limited (TSMC) became the manufacturer of Kodak's digital imaging device, their first CMOS Imaging Sensor (CIS).

What Kodak had created was a Tower of Babylon located in different parts of the world as so many manufacturers had, but now Kodak, like so many others had the challenge of trying to make the pieces fit the needs of a variety of customers. Health services had the potential for major financial growth but that business was not part of the design for printing that Antonio Perez envisioned.

What had looked like a never-ending sales boom in digital cameras began to slide downhill in 2005. Sales that had been to first-time buyers were now showing up as second camera purchasers. Cell phone cameras were slowly building and the announcement of the iPhone in January of 2007 marked the beginning of probably the end of the handheld camera except for limited sales of specialized single lens reflex (SLR) cameras. Cell phone cameras with an eight megapixel imager were becoming common and Nokia had released a 12 Mb camera which brought it to the level of some of the better cameras available today digitally.

Kodak employed statistical modeling in their business research. Trade publications were often more accurate in 2005 to 2007.

Perez expected Kodak to be a $20 billion company by 2010; all of this was to come from three areas of business, health, consumer and commercial imaging. The consumer camera business closed, the health business was sold and little was left of what had been a thriving imaging business.

Some see commercial digital printing as a key and engine of growth. The need for new ways of digitally printing will be a significant potential capital investment for many printers, yet the Internet is providing so much of that advertising capability. In addition, the increased cost of mail along with the decrease of services in the United

States may raise the question whether future printed advertising will be as significant as it was in past years.

The Dayton Operations Division of Kodak was purchased by Cytec in June of 1993 for $70 million (plus an additional amount based on performance). It was sold back to Kodak in January 2004 for $250 million and renamed Kodak Versamark.

Kodak sued Sony for patent infringement on digital cameras and camcorders in 2004. Kodak claimed that Sony infringed 10 patents issued between 1987 and 2003. Sony in turn filed two suits against Kodak. In the end, the company settled with no exchange of money.

At the end of 2004, Kodak agreed to work with IBM to make image sensors for digital cameras and camera phones. In the multiyear partnership, IBM would contribute its semiconductor technology to help Kodak develop sensors with better image quality. The IBM-made sensors were combined with additional technology that Kodak acquired from National Semiconductor Corp. that will allow multi-megapixel image quality and 30 frame/second video in low-light.

One of the first chores that faced Bill Lloyd when he became Chief Technical Officer of Kodak in 2005 was to review the many patents held in Kodak's patent portfolio. Everyone wishes that every patent was perfect or that there were standards to measure patents or the steps in patenting. Certainly there were differences even in those doing the evaluations in the patent office, sometimes very subtle or easy going. Once Lloyd finished, Kodak felt secure in offering licenses or patents for sale.

Kodak learned to live with the fact that no longer would their color film and paper 62-75% margins be a part of their bottom line. More likely 20-30% would be realistic numbers and that does not provide much space for acquisitions or new investments.

Kodak was very late in recognizing that film would not be the cash cow it always had been. Add to that the loss of color paper and chemical business, and Kodak had little left to build on.

The digital camera market, by 2005, was beginning to mature. Analysts indicated that half of the digital camera sales were people who already owned devices and were replacing older models or upgrading. By 2010, shipments of cameras had gone down along with the average selling price and revenue. It was not a healthy situation. Finally, in February 2012, Kodak announced that they would stop making pocket digital cameras. The Apple iPhone and Apple competitive phones had won.

Wall Street fund manager Bill Miller of Leg Mason Value Trust had topped S&P's 500 for 14 years in a row. His feelings were that Kodak's results were bottoming in 2005. Value Trust owned 14% of Kodak which represents 3.4% of the fund's $18 billion in assets. No last minute boosts were expected from Kodak.

Kodak missed its 2005 numbers and planned 10,000 more job cuts.

But by 2005, Kodak had been agile in photography and female-friendly. The company's research showed that women wanted digital photography to be simple and desired high quality prints to share with family and friends. The results were a steady turnaround in Kodak's fortunes—in the digital arena Kodak became number one as seller of digital cameras.

Kodak took on $1.4 billion more in debt to fund its digital acquisitions. Rating agencies Standard & Poor's and Moody's Investor Service lowered Kodak's one-time AAA credit to junk bond status in late April 2005.

It cost Kodak about $980 million to buy Canadian printing-software maker Creo Inc. Creo makes software used by printers to manage the movement of text, graphics, and images from the computer screen to a printing press. Kodak set aside $3 billion for acquisitions partly using funds from actions like eliminating a fifth of its workforce. Graphic communications was one of three pillars that CEO Dan Carp envisioned for Kodak in the digital world.

In the last few years, Perez had been invited to several White House meeting on the economy, diversity or just for social events. On Super Bowl weekend 2010, Perez flew to Washington, DC on his corporate jet for a White House social event. His plane was parked in a hanger at Dulles Airport.

The heavy snows that night caused the roof of the hanger to collapse on Perez's plane. A few folks like myself who have a religious bend said, "God sent a message to Antonio, but we are not sure he was listening." The plane was a total loss. Perhaps Perez might have to fly commercially to Spain to visit his family regularly instead of in a company jet.

In the spring of 2011, a Wal-Mart store in Joplin, Missouri, was destroyed by a devastating tornado that swept through the area. In November, the tore had a grand opening celebration and Fujifilm offered to restore damaged photographs and to have new family portraits made, free of charge. Fuji was hopeful that their efforts would help create new memories for the Joplin community. Once upon a time, Kodak would have sent immediate help to the storm area. Those days have gone forever as Kodak protected its very existence.

Chapter Nine—Is There a Future for Kodak?

For tomorrow, the question remains, will there be a Kodak? Little remains of the Kodak that was. The large print engines that had begun to appear from Kodak will compete with companies with products that have already been proven and are currently successfully installed. The home inkjet printer business is shaky at best. No buyers have come forth to acquire Kodak's many patents, and when they are gone, what will replace them?

We have spoken here of Kodak's "Culture". Is it a state of mind on the part of employees or something more than that? In Kodak's case it was loyalty and faith that began with the opening of the company by George Eastman and the sharing with employees of not only information but also of the earnings of the company. Today, these are gone. Culture, in the case of Kodak, also came in the pride that Rochester and New York State have had for more than 100 years in one of the largest companies in its field within United States and in foreign countries.

Today, this culture is fragmented and fits very well the description of the children's Humpty Dumpty whose pieces could not be put back together. The Kodak that many of us knew is gone forever. The memories may be a book of photos that, if there is an emergency, will be one of the first things we take from our home. Or it may be a form of digital memory that we will not only keep and protect but even send it to outside sources to store and preserve for us.

Will the greatness and original sense of purpose driven by George Eastman return to the Eastman Kodak Company? The last seven chiefs of the company have not brought Kodak back to its preeminent role as the world leader in imaging.

Perhaps we should ask the question, what is an image? At this very instant you are looking at an image–perhaps it's a page on a flat-panel display, maybe even your telephone, it may even be a paper book page. Image may be a picture or more formally a photograph that you could be looking at not printed on paper, on the screen, or even projected in air. Perhaps the day will come when images will be projected directly to the brain – you have to ask the classic question, "Why not?"

Images are the story of our lives, records, medical factoids, or even scratches of a pen or pencil.

Can Kodak be brought back to its original imaging roots? Some will say it will never happen, others will say it is too late, yet perhaps, someone may simply say, why not? Perhaps there's a young Mark Zuckerberg, Bill Gates, Steve Jobs out there who will take up the torch.

The end might also be marked by the large round stone that sits off Lake Avenue in Rochester surrounded by beautiful flowering Japanese trees—where George Eastman is buried.

The opportunity is there, who will take it? Perhaps another great visionary leader will appear. It may not be that easy in today's global society balancing vision, consumers and the financial challenges of today's quarter-to-quarter financial demands.

Kodak's manufacturing sites have shrunk almost as fast as its payroll, a not unexpected consequence. The largest equipment manufacturing site, Elmgrove, has been sold and is now struggling to become a technology park.

The famous Kodak Park has become a true grassy park since almost five dozen buildings were razed or sold. Once it was possible to take a tour of the giant 1200 acre Kodak Park where many film and paper products were manufactured, but these tours are gone along with many of the original buildings.

Kodak Park is now called Eastman Park. Maybe someday it will be a people park provided that the ground pollution of over 100 years of manufacturing can be cleaned up successfully. Kodak has been the focus of many years of concern by environmentalists. Maybe all that will be left at Eastman Park one day will be the burial site of George Eastman.

During the first 90 years in business, the Eastman Kodak Company became a household word and Kodak was the world's leader when it came to inventions related to imaging. From the time of the earliest Brownie cameras, even George Eastman himself had to be careful that the word 'Kodak' did not slip into everyday language, losing one of the great trademarks. Legal barriers caused by patent infringements, antitrust, and consumer activism began to cast long shadows over Kodak and took a toll on the company. Feet of clay could be easily stepped on and broken.

Kodak Brand Ranking

	Brand Rank	($ mil)	Change
2000		11,822	
2001	27	10,801	-9%
2002	30	9,671	-10%
2003	34	7,826	-19%
2004	53	5,231	-33%
2005	62	4,979	-5%
2006	70	4,406	-12%
2007	82	3,874	-12%

Kodak's brand value declined. According to Interbrand, after 2007, Kodak was no longer a top 100 brand.

The brand is the most important asset that a company has. As technology shifts, the brand becomes increasingly more important to the company. What has happened is with the changes at Kodak, its brand, while still present all over the world, does not evoke the kind of reaction, emotional reaction, awareness that it did two or three decades ago or even five years ago.

Recently, a lawyer friend was conducting a class for junior high school students in Florida. The class was covering the battles of World War II and readily showed how little these young people knew about that. He also

112

asked them if they knew what the word Kodak meant? Not one student was able to identify Kodak, its products or its business. It was a sad note that the word Kodak has slipped so badly.

One afternoon in the fall of 2003, I sat down with a man I had known for 20 years, Minoru Ohnishi, chairman of Fujifilm in his office in Tokyo. In the 1970s, he and his company recognized that the digital challenge would occur. Many of these young technical people were discussing it and a Fuji Device Research Center was established in the United States to both do research and obtain technologies so that Fuji could grow.

While Ohnishi himself is not technical, his senior managing director at the time, Hirozo Ueda, Ohnishi's Senior Managing Director, now retired, did a good job of putting the needed pieces together to support the future growth of digital products and services.

Ueda did much of the work in setting up programs and locations for factories for digital production. Ohnishi ended our conversation with his hope that all 6 billion people in the world would enjoy photography because it was to become more convenient, affordable, and easier to use thanks to technology advancements from companies like his. I had met a wise man with great vision.

If you talk to people who have visited Japan often, they see Japan and particularly Fujifilm surviving. While Kodak flounders, Fujifilm survives and grows. They have a long-term vision and they have done many things early which were far-reaching.

For example, they knew the digital technology was going to be part of the future, so they formed a design team and developed expertise in the design of semiconductor sensors. They also created a significant manufacturing plant in Sendai which provided their own manufactured sensors for consumer cameras as well as printed circuit board (PCB) and full camera production. In this way, they have design control over the sensor which is the camera part of film and gives much more freedom in designing.

Kodak never had any state-of-the-art PCB facility. Most small boards that Kodak made were for film camera auto exposure systems because outside vendors were too expensive.

Fujifilm has retained technology control by investing in expertise in a design shop, far away from their basic business. Applications designed for professionals or consumers did not need to use the designs for other manufacturer's sensors. Kodak forgot that the sensor was the equivalent of film—something that Kodak knew a great deal about.

Arrogance, unfortunately, flows from pride and Kodak's past successes gave it good reason for pride. Kodachrome is an awesome technology and only one of many film products for both still and motion photography that Kodak designed over the years. But there were many recent failures. But the arrogance, especially of managers, did not bode well with customers of others who interfaced with the company.

A friend of mine recently talked to the inventor of the computer mouse, Douglas Engelbart. Engelbart thought that we had made computers too simple—the philosophy of serving the lowest common denominator. A lot more is possible from computers than we have seen so far.

The purpose of the Corporation is not to exist as an entity. The role is to maximize shareholders return.

Shareholders invest a lot of money in a company and the whole purpose of the company is to give the owners a decent return. That is the function of the company. This is a different trade-off between stakeholders and shareholders. Yes, shareholders have the residual claim to the Corporation.

After everybody else gets their fair due, if there is anything left over, that's what goes to the shareholders. So you have to pay your taxes, your suppliers, your employers, making a decent place for employees to work or you won't get any employees, and you have community responsibilities.

When you go through the corporation, you tick off all the different claimants on a company and they all have either specific legal claims like taxes and community responsibilities like Community Chest or United Way or things that will make the community more attractive, to bring better employees to work for you. Then you look at things like advertising and R&D, so that the future value brought back to the present is as large as can be. You certainly don't want to overspend or underspend.

If you take a company, as many do today, and look at it only financially, forgotten are the dimensions that have developed in the case of a company like Kodak over 100 years. There is a richness of their own development but it is fragile as we have seen with companies like General Electric, General Motors, Bausch & Lomb, Xerox, and others. This gets you to a point of company reality.

Kodak would not have to look far to find an example of a company that has used its core competencies effectively for more than 150 years. Corning Inc. is a short drive from Rochester and has created core competencies that they have been willing to shed in favor of original core competencies that needed further development.

From Corning original glass came as large sheet glass for flat screen television sets. A glass with great strength, Gorilla Glass, has become the glass choice for watches, telephones and now large versions of it are serving on huge LCD or OLED panels. They offer both strength and lightness. Yet Corning was willing to give up lines like Steuben Glass which no longer was profitable or in great demand. Corning had the strength to change, yet it was always on the alert for new or renewed opportunities.

Is there a brand loyalty around the Kodak brand name? It certainly lasted for many years but the young people involved in the digital market of today do not even recognize the word Kodak.

Kodak provided a "poster-boy" backdrop for the destruction of American jobs, spiraling health costs, pensions, and a vanishing middle class.

In *Print 2020*, a special research report from the Rochester Institute of Technology, researchers saw fewer printers but bigger printing houses with electronic paper, and the new screen technology. Compared to 1998, their prediction of tons of paper indicates a 20% increase.

The processing laboratories that develop camera films shot for Hollywood movies are also the same laboratories that developed the prints that will be shown in theaters around the world. The business of camera film and print film and the movie industry has been major revenue producers for Kodak.

Published reports indicate that film prints for theater release will end in 2013. This will dramatically alter Kodak's film production operations.

Theater Management Systems was another new area for Kodak. It was an opportunity to be a major player in the coming digital movie arena. One of their first sales was of 200 digital cinema systems. Customers were impressed with both the concept and Kodak technology.

People within Kodak recognized the move in theaters from film projection to digital projection. Kodak had developed a theater laser projector system covered by some 50 US patents that was ready to be introduced to banks for financing in 2009. With the difficult financial times, the banks pulled out and self-financing by Kodak was no longer possible. The product was to have been announced in 2011 with actual product shipping in 2012. It may become another lost business.

Kodak had great technology but Kodak's weak financial position made it difficult to proceed with new opportunities. With announcements from sources in Hollywood that film prints to theaters would end in 2013, the Kodak Laser Projector and the 50 patents covering it may become a significant piece of intellectual property, but it would be even better if it could be an ongoing stream of revenue to keep Kodak in the movie business supplying theater equipment.

Kodak's future in the world of imaging has been significantly challenged by people of imagination like the late Steve Jobs and others. The invention of the charge coupled device (CCD) almost 50 years ago dramatically changed the world of imaging as much as George Eastman's work with plates and roll film changed photography. Is there a place for a company like Eastman Kodak Company?

While some marketing and management gurus will suggest that Kodak should focus on a single product or area, Kodak has already wasted both time and energy like a bouncing ball. Over 40 years of Kodak CEOs has not produced a single visionary or significant leader. Kodak Board of Directors needs to share the responsibility for their lack of vision in their selection of Kodak leaders.

Maybe it is time for a turnaround from discussions of the early 1990s when Kodak talked briefly about buying Apple in the time of John Sculley. Today, with Apple's billion dollar cash hoard, how much would it take to buy a company worth just over $650 million? Kodak comes complete with over 1000 patents providing intellectual property that might finally be used as well as good people who might become people in the mold of the hard-working people of Apple.

The day may come when Apple stores around the world may have a Kodak department again teaching people how to do more with the digital cameras in their iPhones and iPads or take them up another notch to a camera that can do sports photography and other things not dreamt of today.

"Disruptive" technologies like digital in its many forms may not meet the needs or likes of some core customers and may not be profit generators. The innovators sell to the customers that they can develop their product further and suddenly, to the surprise of the supplier, they now have a major competitor to contend with. That is the world we live in today.

Senior people who moved on to other companies from Kodak had a lot to give. Patricia Russo, who joined Lucent, said about her people, "This team is very clear-eyed about what works and what has yet to be done." Bob Keegan, who joined Goodyear after running Kodak's Consumer group, brought a greater understanding of consumer habits to Goodyear.

Kodak can be a model of a reborn 100 year old company. Where is the leader who is ready for the challenge?

Goodbye to our friend, the Kodak of old! We hope there is a new Kodak with a new awakening that will carry on that great name with inventive products and profitability.

www.ingramcontent.com/pod-product-compliance
Lightning Source LLC
Chambersburg PA
CBHW051328170526
45166CB00002B/722